Children in care

Needs, challenges and evidence

Edited by Terry Philpot

Children in care: Needs, challenges and evidence

Edited by Terry Philpot

The authors have asserted their rights in accordance with the *Copyright, Designs and Patents Act (1988)* to be identified as the authors of their chapters.

Published in 2023 by:

Step Beach Press Ltd
28 Osborne Villas
Hove
East Sussex
BN3 2RE

Email: info@stepbeachpress.co.uk
Web: www.stepbeachpress.co.uk

This book is published in association with Five Rivers, a leading social enterprise providing therapeutic services for children in care for education, assessment and therapy, crisis intervention, and residential and foster care. Founded in 1989, Five Rivers has supported thousands of children with adverse childhood experiences to work through their developmental, attachment and trauma experiences through the specialist care and therapeutic practices. Five Rivers provides consistent high quality social impact in the children's lives and their communities.

A catalogue record for this book is available from the British Library.

ISBN: 978-1-908779-60-1

Editor: Terry Philpot

Cover design: Step Beach Press

Page layout and typesetting: karenhobden.com for Step Beach Press

Printing: L&S Printing Co Ltd, West Sussex, England

Editor's note

Sadly, Ann Buchanan, one of our authors, died before this book was published. Indeed, her chapter on residential care was delivered only weeks before her unexpected death in February 2022, while on holiday. It is likely the last piece she wrote for publication.

Details of her life and achievements can be found in the Obituary published in *The Guardian*, 13 May 2022 (available online at www.theguardian.com/society/2022/may/13/ann-buchanan-obituary).

Contents

List of Contributors

Ann Buchanan was Senior Research Associate at the Department of Social Policy and Intervention at Oxford University and Professor Emerita of Social Work. Before becoming an academic she spent 10 years working as a social worker in an inner city. At Oxford she set up the Centre for Research into Parenting and Children and undertook studies on parenting, fathering, grandfathering, sibling relations and child well-being. Some of her earliest studies were on children who were looked after, using both national longitudinal data sets to track what happened to children in care, and studies that gave voice to the young people who were being looked after. Later in her career, she worked with Barnardo's and Research in Practice co-writing a book for social workers in 2004 with Charlotte Ritchie titled *What Works for Troubled Children*. She travelled extensively and lectured on her work across the world. Her last book (co-edited with Anna Rotkirch) was *Brothers and Sisters: Sibling relationships across the life course* (2021, published by Macmillan). She died in February 2022.

Antonella Cirasola is a qualified clinical psychologist registered at both the Italian Council of Psychologists and the UK Health & Care Professions Council. She holds a BSc and MSc in Clinical Psychology from Sapienza University and an MSc in Psychoanalytic Developmental Psychology from University College London (UCL). She also completed a funded PhD at the UCL Psychoanalysis Unit on the role of the therapeutic alliance in the treatment of adolescent depression. She works as a clinical practitioner within the School Remote Service at the Anna Freud Centre and as Module Lead and Senior Research Tutor at UCL. Her research interests are psychotherapy process and outcome; attachment and therapeutic alliance; and trauma and mental health.

Richard Cross is Head of Assessment and Therapy for Five Rivers Child Care. He began his work with children, young people and adults who have experienced significant adversity and complex trauma in 1991. He has developed and piloted numerous relational therapeutic programs to meet the needs of children and young people, from his first group work approach in Scotland for adolescents to addressing sexually harmful behaviour; to developing the advanced EQUIP (a program designed to meet the needs of anti-social youth with severe conduct disorder) in New Zealand; and to bringing trauma-informed care to the UK through the Sanctuary Model in 2006. He specialises in complex trauma and dissociative disorders and frequently offers training internationally to qualified mental health professionals. He is a fellow and faculty member of the world's oldest society for trauma and dissociation, the International Society for Trauma & Dissociation, and a faculty member of the Arizona Trauma Institute. His research aims to improve understanding of what works in assessment and interventions for children and young people who have experienced significant adversity. He is also a Director of the Bowlby Centre, London and the Institute of Recovery from Children Trauma.

Chris Hanvey was the Chief Executive of the Royal College of Paediatrics and Child Health and, prior to this, was the Deputy Chief Executive of Barnardo's and Chief Executive of the Thomas Coram Foundation. His career has spanned posts in local government and health, the voluntary sector and the Cabinet Office. He was a Non-executive Director of the Devon Clinical Commissioning Group, chairing the quality committee and being lead on safeguarding. He was also vice-chair of the Department of Education's Family Fund and is both a Fellow of the Royal Society of Arts and the Dartington Social Policy Unit for children. He is author of several books and numerous articles. His latest book is *Shaping Children's Services* (2019, published by Routledge).

Saul Hillman is a Senior Research Fellow at the Anna Freud Centre and an honorary lecturer at University College London. He teaches and supervises across several different postgraduate programmes at both institutions. Within his research role, he has primarily managed and worked on studies around attachment and mentalization. Much of his work has been in the field of children who were either looked-after or adopted. He has a specific interest in measure development following on from completing a PhD on the Story Stem Assessment Profile. He also works as a research consultant for a number of other charities and organisations. He is also a qualified integrative therapist. His research interests and attachment; mentalization; measure development; and looked-after children and adoption.

Richard Machin is a Senior Lecturer in Social Work and Health at Nottingham Trent University. He teaches social policy on a range of courses including social work, health and social care and public health.

His area of expertise is social security and welfare rights. Before moving into academia, he worked for many years as a case worker and manager in a local authority welfare rights team and maintains links to this sector by giving freelance training for the Child Poverty Action Group. He has published in Critical Social Policy, Disability and Society, Social Work and Social Sciences Review, Journal of Social Welfare and Family Law, and Ethics and Social Welfare.

Pam McConnell is the Chief Executive of Five Rivers, which she founded in 1989. She qualified as a social worker with a dual qualification in social policy and administration and the Certificate in Social Work from Coventry University, and continued professional training as a psychotherapist, group analyst, and family therapist. She specialised in child protection and mental health in families with vulnerable children, working in the London Boroughs of Chiswick and Croydon and with the NSPCC in Wiltshire and then became an independent expert in the courts. As a result of seeing that the experience of being in not able to deliver a therapeutic experience to children, she began her first therapeutic children's home in 1989. This led to a progression onto other associated services for children in care, namely education, fostering and direct therapy and research and training.

Perdita Mousley is an educational leader with over 20 years' experience within a variety of educational, residential and health settings for children, young people and adults with additional and complex needs. As well as being a qualified teacher, she holds qualifications in educational leadership and special educational needs. She has a particular interest in inclusion and supporting learners with additional needs in particular autism and dyslexia. Most recently, her work includes educational research and consultancy. Previous to this, she was an executive director for a national charity with overall responsibility for education, therapy and residential care within independent special schools and colleges; she also led day care services within the high secure hospital sector. Dr Mousley has successfully developed services from inception through to delivery, including independent special schools and children's homes. She has led national projects to raise awareness of mental health as well as leading research on the educational experiences of looked-after children.

Fungisai Mushawa has been A Senior Social Work Lecturer at Nottingham Trent University since 2017. She is the Course Lead for the BA Social Work Course and has teaching duties across the undergraduate, postgraduate and continual progressional development programmes in social work. Her interest in research is related to work with children and families and issues that affect black communities. Her publications have been centred around work with black sub-Saharan communities. She has practice experience in generic social work whilst working in Zimbabwe where she qualified as a social worker, and in the UK, social work with children and families including working with foster carers and children in foster placements from social worker to managerial level. She then worked as a fostering independent reviewing officer and social work consultant before moving on to higher education.

Paula Oliveira is a Senior Research Fellow at the Anna Freud National Centre for Children and Families, working across several research projects involving vulnerable children and families, such as children in care or at risk of entering care. She also teaches applied developmental neuroscience and developmental psychopathology in the developmental neuroscience and psychopathology research Masters, a UCL programme that runs in partnership with the Anna Freud Centre and Yale University. Previously, she undertook psychology training at University of Minho in Portugal and a Masters in clinical psychology. She then completed a PhD in psychology at UCL, researching institutionalised children with attachment disorders and other socio–emotional difficulties. After that she worked on a randomised controlled trial to adapt a parenting intervention for children in foster care with symptoms of attachment disorder. Her research has been focused on attachment, attachment disorders and neurodevelopment among children in care.

Terry Philpot is a writer and journalist. He is the author or editor of 23 books, including ones on adoption, fostering, the voluntary sector, and sex offenders. His most recent books books are *31 London Cemeteries to Visit Before You Die* (2012); *Beside the Seaside: Brighton's Places and its People* (2015); *Secret Lewes* (2017); *Secret Rye* (2017); *Secret Aldeburgh to Southwold* (2018); and *Over Here, Over There: The People and the Places that Made the Story of London and America* (2019). His book, *III Literary Sights in London that You Shouldn't Miss*, will be published next year. He has contributed 23 entries to the *Oxford Dictionary of National Biography* and writes and reviews regularly for *The Tablet*, while contributing to *The Guardian*, *The Times* and the *Daily Telegraph*. A former editor, he has won several awards for journalism. He has been a trustee of the Social Care Institute for Excellence, the Centre Policy on Ageing, the Cardinal Hume Centre, and Circles UK. He has volunteered with Circles UK and Human Writes, and presently volunteers for New Bridge and as a tour guide at the Weiner Holocaust Library, London.

John Pierson moved from the US to Britain in the early 1970s. He taught courses with the Workers Education Association and Sussex University Extra-mural Department, before working with the Richmond Fellowship. He subsequently qualified as a social worker at Liverpool University and joined Cheshire social services department as a field worker with children and families, and later as service manager. Moving into academia he taught at Staffordshire University for 30 years on courses covering childcare law, the evolution of the welfare state, and community development. He is the author of several books including, *Understanding Social Work: History and Context* (2012), *Tackling Social Exclusion and Poverty* (2016), and *A New History of Social Work: Values and Practice in the Struggle for Social Justice* (2022). He retired in 2021 but continues to research how and why social work philosophies change over time, and to help at the local youth centre where he has volunteered for the last 20 years.

Richard Rose is the Director of Therapeutic Life Story Work International, which provides consultancy and training on therapeutic life story work and working with hard-to-reach children and adolescents, and develops academic training programmes in the UK and Internationally. He has worked with traumatised children and families since he was 17 years old, and over the last 40 years his direct work with hurt children and young people is still at the heart of his working life. He works with organisations across the world promoting best practice. He is an adjunct Associate Professor of Social Work and Social Policy at La Trobe University, Melbourne, an Honorary Associate of Berry Street, Melbourne, and an Honorary Associate of the Open Adoption Institute, University of Sydney. He works with the Department of Human Services, Oregon, USA, and ORPARC (Adoption Services), and is a Clinical Complex Case Consultant for the child protection services in Australian Capital Territories; he provides similar services to social care teams across the globe. Richard Rose is the author (with Terry Philpot) of *The Child's Own Story: Life Story Work with Traumatised Children* (2004); *Life Story Therapy with Traumatised Children: A Model for Practice* (2012); and *Innovative Therapeutic Life Story Work* (2017).

Jennifer E. Simpson is a Senior Lecturer in Social Work and Course Leader for MA Advanced Social Work in the Department of Social Work, Care and Community at Nottingham Trent University (NTU). Her social work practice background is fostering; it was her interest in this area that led her to undertake a PhD focusing on how children in care use mobile devices and social media to stay in touch with their families.

She has also carried out research spanning social media and social work; child, adult and family social work and services; as well as higher education continual professional development for integrated social services workforces. She now teaches a variety of continuing professional development (CPD) modules as the course leader for NTU's advanced social work course.

Simon Ward is a Senior Lecturer in Social Work at Liverpool John Moores University. He is a registered social worker and has worked in various positions, as a social worker and team manager, mostly within local authority services and especially with children in care and in court settings. He is Vice-chair of a national voluntary organisation's regional fostering panel. His 'second' career is teaching social work and social policy with The Open University, University of Manchester, Staffordshire University and LJMU.

Foreword

Pam McConnell

Five Rivers Child Care is a social care and social enterprise organisation, which offers therapeutic children's services with clinical, education provision alongside our residential homes and fostering families. We are dedicated to providing services to children and young people in need, creating an environment that nurtures and guides them to a meaningful future.

We rely on three main ways of supporting development of our work and expertise:

1. The first is the use of evidence-based practice.

2. Second, we have feedback loops by which consultation with the client or child at the end of a session or completion of treatment and the like help us to know whether intervention has been helpful.

3. Third, there are lessons learned reviews, whereby, without apportioning blame, we learn what has gone wrong, what the errors were, and sequences of events leading up to them, and how this can be prevented or, at least, risks reduced by any additional steps. This process would usually be written up and reviewed as a systemic review to improve services while at the same time lowering risks and educating people on the potential errors.

A book such as this one is a good way to share good practice: it is a way that brings together the latest thinking in policy and practice we now have on how to help children. At a time when there is the highest level of concern about the vulnerability of children, with more mental health concerns being reported than ever before (1), this book has many useful insights to help them.

Each chapter has been written by an expert in their field, with a level of experience in working with those providing services to children in the care system or who are in need. The book offers the latest important research affecting, in particular, looked-after children, that should be helpful for carers, residential and therapeutic staff, youth workers, teachers and teaching assistants, psychologists and psychiatrists. It will be of interest, too, to birth parents, step-parents, and adoptive parents, all of whom want to know what is changing in what we know about how children can have the best chances of doing well, and achieving their potential.

Children who are not in care may also suffer disruption in their families, have to move, cope with sudden loss of people close to them, or have had poor attachment in their early months and years, or suffer trauma within or outside the family.

There have been two major areas of information where there has been great change over the last 20 years, change that affects our daily lives and our thinking about what both we and children need. First, there is our ability to understand the brain through MRI scanning, which is now more widely and cheaply available; in addition to this, our building on earlier work has led to neuroscience being one of the fastest-growing areas of study.

MRI scans have exploded myths such as 'we only use ten per cent of our brain' – in fact, we use all of our brain in different ways and in different patterns at different times. Previously, it was believed that the number of brain cells in our bodies was fixed and that once they started dying they were not replaced – we now know that they can regenerate. We know, too, that there are a small number of areas in the brain that are responsible for specific functions. Thus, the brain is far more complex and interconnected than had hitherto been believed.

We now talk of plasticity and that we can 're-wire' our brains through play and creativity, by changing what we say to ourselves, what we do, what habits we develop. This means many things that were thought of as fixed, are not. At its centre, this means that all of us can change and be radically different because we *decide* to behave differently. What an important message to give children – that no matter what has happened to them in their lives, they can become the authors of their own script and their own destiny.

The second part of the truly radical change in our information about people is our knowledge of positive psychology. It used to be that studies focused on what was wrong with people or children and how to put it right. Now we ask ourselves: why do some people do well and thrive, and how can we help make this work with more people, more of the time? This has led to strengths-based work. So now we know that for children to thrive, they need praise but also they need to believe in themselves, to have a 'growth mindset', to be able to fail but to persist, to figure things out. As Dweck and Yeager (2019) explain:

> 'In a growth mindset, people believe that their most basic abilities can be developed through dedication and hard work – brains and talent are just the starting point. This view creates a love of learning and a resilience that is essential for great accomplishment.' (2)

We now know that we solve problems better by thinking positively – about what we can do – and that we can train ourselves to this; we are not just destined by our genetic inheritance or the circumstances into which we were born and how we were nurtured.

These new structures help our understanding of learning and teaching and of replacing negative and harmful patterns of behaviour with new and helpful ones. We know that we can teach children through play and that is the most effective way to help them learn and practise their new behaviours.

We are undergoing a revolution in our understanding of the importance of nutrition and exercise – for children as well as adults. So many assumptions were being made 15 to 20 years ago, for example, that children were 'busy' and active so they didn't need exercise. Now we recognise that the more sedentary nature of our lifestyles changes our brains, too; reduced movement can lead to complicated long-term chronic illnesses which need to be mitigated with proper planned food and exercise for children of all ages. It is a great way to help manage mood, sleep, learning and social relationships. It is part of creating a child who is resilient and able to cope with different life stresses.

Against these positive developments is the context of how society looks after its children in need. Perhaps it can be summed up as well-intentioned but based in a heavily regulated, inflexible and, therefore, expensive regime. The ability to create normal parenting boundaries is not allowed without resorting to a judge making a decision. These rules are over-powering and professionals working with looked-after children and those in difficulty are often confronted by angry, mistrustful, suspicious, colleagues in related professions, and anxious parents. Suddenly, everyone is an expert with an opinion and these prejudices are imposed on children's lives and the decisions made for them. Much of it is based on the adults' own family experiences and how they personally believe children *should* be cared for, rather than what is established good practice, based on evidence and research.

Divisions that exist between the health service and social care children's services and education increase the challenges as they have with other client groups, and these divisions create not only create poor experiences but unnecessary waste, delays, and demotivation.

There are many new approaches to helping children that have been developed, in addition to psychotherapy, drama, art, and music therapy, that reflect the concept of creating therapies that can be activated by individuals who know themselves what they need. That is, help that is therapeutic and can be delivered by non-experts, who have specific techniques and the ability to encourage taking regular and active steps to improve mood, sleep, social connection, confidence, and reducing anxiety and depression.

This book, we hope, not only answers many of the questions which affect children's lives and services, but also seeks to show how we can shape the services that help and encourage children. This is, as our authors show, what children need in terms of therapy, their education, and their physical, emotional and mental health, and, generally, the need to be able to lead fulfilling and positively-focused lives. Importantly, as a theme which runs through this book, it is important to emphasise what children in care and other troubled children *can* do rather than what they cannot do, and how they can be encouraged to succeed. We need to recognise that their aspirations – as children and in their future adult lives – are very little different from those more fortunate than themselves.

References

(1)   One in six children aged 5 to 16 were identified as having a probable mental health problem in July 2021, an increase from one in nine in 2017. That's five children in every classroom. (www.youngminds.org)

(2)   Dweck, C. S. and Yeager, D. S. (2019) 'Mindsets: a view from two eras', *Perspect. Psychol. Sci.* 14, 481–496.

CHAPTER 1

How Did We Get Here? Residential Care, Then and Now: A Historical Perspective

John Pierson

Introduction

This chapter offers a short account of a long and continuing story: the development of public and voluntary care of children. It begins with life in the workhouse in the midst of the upheaval of the industrial revolution and ends with the transformed care sector of the 21st century. The aim is to give some insight into the evolving nature of that care. If it awakens readers to the importance of this history the chapter will have done its work.

Children under the poor law: the workhouse and boarding out

We begin with a Britain preoccupied with the social consequences of the industrial revolution: mass migration from country to city, fast-growing manufacturing districts with the working families living in cheaply built, overcrowded housing while trying to make ends meet in a wholly new kind of labour market. The 'old' Poor Law in England and Wales that had largely supported destitute families in their local parish for more than two centuries in a largely rural economy, did not function in the densely populated towns and cities that were coming into being. In its place, in 1834, Parliament created a new system based on poor law unions in England and Wales, each run by a board of guardians and overseen by the Poor Law Commission in London.

The New Poor Law (as it came to be called) enabled unions to 'relieve' families who had no means of subsistence. Each union was required to build a workhouse – the key to welfare reform, 1830s-style. Parliament, concerned that able-bodied labourers would claim support they did not need, intended that day-to-day life in 'the house' be unappealing. The standard of living, in food, accommodation and daily routine, was purposely below that of the lowest paid able-bodied worker so that only the truly destitute on the edge of starvation would turn to it for help – the so-called 'workhouse test'. This would deter claiming and divide the poor between the 'undeserving' and the 'deserving'.

Children came into workhouses by the tens of thousands for three reasons. First, because they were deserted or orphaned (including 'half-orphaned' children with one parent deceased and the other in prison or asylum, long term). Second, they came as children of a family with no income. Third, they were children whose parents were unable to afford to look after them – they were the children from large families, with impoverished widows or unmarried mothers, either pregnant or with infants. Throughout the 19th century half of the children in workhouses fell into that first category – deserted and on their own.

Contemporaries observed that children coming into 'the house' were smaller, sicker, more prone to disease, with little confidence in themselves. One Poor Law inspector answerable to the Poor Law Board in London, noted that they were '…scrofulous, undersized, badly-developed, narrow-chested, degenerate class … torpid and flaccid in mind and body' (1). Contagious and infectious diseases – ringworm, ophthalmia, measles and scarlet fever – came with them.

Poor Law authorities wrestled with the contradictions between providing a reasonable environment for children while maintaining an unappealing regime for adults and cost efficiency. Children's quarters, separate from adults, lacked stimulation as many Poor Law inspectors noted. Children could only go out when accompanied by a workhouse officer; young children had no individual toys and even more generous minded unions were not allowed to provide toys and books at Christmas but had to rely on voluntary donations.

Charles Shaw remembered his admission as an 8-year-old to the Chell workhouse in the Potteries when his family hit rock bottom in 1842, a year of exceptional economic distress. He noted:

'Everybody we saw and spoke to looked metallic, as if worked from within by a hidden machinery. Their voices were metallic, and sounded harsh and imperative.'

Shaw was shown to a cellar where he was washed and given workhouse clothes (2):

'Nobody asked us if we were tired, or if we had had any breakfast.'

There were undoubtedly instances of cruel punishments. Shaw gives a harrowing account of the flogging of a boy with other boys having to watch. The Poor Law inspectorate in London opposed corporal punishment from the start urging that discipline should be enforced through withdrawal of privileges such as a favourite meal, with confinement or flogging only with permission of the guardians. But it proved difficult to stamp out. As one inspector put it (3):

'under a proper system of education corporal punishment need not and ought not to be resorted to… but I apprehend that the class of persons who are likely to fill the office of union [workhouse] school masters is very far removed from the intelligence and discretion that can alone supersede the now ordinary methods of correction.'

Workhouse schools were separate from the workhouse – in the worst, the 'teacher' was simply an older, untrained resident 'pauper' who did little more than look after children. In better funded schools, English history, geography, grammar, literacy, and arithmetic were offered, as reports from national inspectors confirm. Workhouse infirmaries were even in advance of their time. Poor Law medical officers and nurses, increasingly organised as a profession, became experts in contagion and childhood diseases, setting up separate children's wards, then a new development in hospital paediatric care (4).

Some unions pooled budgets to form district schools. Dubbed 'barrack schools' in the press because pupils slept in large dormitories, they offered training in a trade such as tailoring, shoemaking, carpentry, and blacksmith work. Girls were offered sewing, mending, cooking and training for household service. Despite early enthusiasm they soon established their own institutional environment with lessons, meal times and bed times strictly controlled by the clock. In the majority, underwear was held in common, walks out happened on Sundays, and attention to individual pupils was non-existent.

Boarding out

The impact of industrialisation in Scotland was intensive. The rapid depopulation of rural areas (assisted by Highland clearances) overcrowded cities and produced brutal working conditions that surpassed those in England. In the mid1840s, a Poor Law for Scotland replaced a wholly voluntary system of assistance controlled by kirk and landowners that had been patchy at best. New parochial boards were given the power to assist the destitute, like the unions in England and Wales, but were more parsimonious and remained under the control of parish officials. Unlike the English unions, parochial boards heavily favoured boarding children with 'stranger' households. Since the aim was to separate children from parents, who would otherwise pass on contaminating behaviours such as idleness and alcoholism (5), children were placed in distant, rural areas. These included the Western islands and Highlands – alien land for the impoverished children of Glasgow, Dundee and Edinburgh. There was little concern for supervision nor a system of inspection as in England. By 1910, 90 per cent of children under the Scottish Poor Law were boarded out – or 7,000 children annually (6).

Unions in England and Wales approached boarding out more cautiously. Not until 1870 were Poor Law unions allowed to place children with foster families. Placements were long term, children remaining with their foster family until age 14 when they left for an apprenticeship or domestic service and were no longer legally defined as a child. Because boarding out was presumed to cut ties with the child's family, regulations in England and Wales prescribed that only deserted or orphaned children, or children with a parent in prison or asylum long term could be boarded out in deference to parental rights.

The risk of harm to boarded-out children was another reason why English unions were cautious in their placement practice. Marianne Mason, who was, from 1885, Chief Inspector of boarded-out children in England and Wales, regularly testified before parliamentary committees on the children she found beaten and bruised in her placement visits (7):

> 'It is very seldom I go a month without finding an illtreated child, a really ill-treated child.'

Regulations compelled each union to establish a visiting committee to supervise placements. Mason accelerated the role of women in visiting fostered children declaring that only women 'can properly investigate the conditions of girls yet it often happens that two or three guardians, gentlemen, will visit the place[ment] for the purpose' (8).

Evangelical voluntary organisations

Poor Law officials had no power to search out homeless or deserted children on the streets of urban Britain – 'gutter children' or 'street Arabs' in the parlance of the day. This was the cause that evangelical reformers took up in the late 1860s, adding an important dimension to residential care as they did so. Believing that children learned their sense of responsibility and moral duty in the family, they poured energy, time and organisation into rescuing children from dissolute, neglectful, 'vicious' families in slums before they were 'contaminated' by their surroundings.

For Thomas Barnardo, the work of saving souls – his own as well as others – was the means to realize his Christian faith. While he declared no child would be turned away from the homes he founded, he treated children's parents and relatives as obstacles to his mission (9).

Thomas Stephenson, a Methodist, also spoke in missionary terms but in founding the first National Children's Home his belief in the need to reach the souls of the children in his care was less pronounced than Barnardo's – and, unlike Barnardo, he accepted children after discussion with their parents with his records noting parents' neglect but also their virtues (10).

The evangelical rescue mission reached its extreme in the emigration societies that sent children to Canada and other colonies from the late 1860s on. Barnardo's homes accounted for nearly a quarter of all emigrants (11). William Quarrier, a Scottish Baptist, also enthusiastically supported emigration. Within nine months of opening his first children's home in 1871 he had a party of 35 children ready to sail to Canada. His biographer relates how the staff hugged and prayed with the children on their eve of departure, convinced that emigration was morally right and in the children's best interests (12). The Poor Law administration in London, doubting the glowing publicity from the emigration societies themselves, sent Andrew Doyle, one of its inspectors, to Canada to investigate. His landmark report noted how children in placement had been lost sight of through lax supervision, poor record keeping, and exploitation on Canadian farms (13). The emigration societies, with powerful political connections, successfully counter attacked and the practice continued for another 90 years; not until the 1980s would the scale of the trauma for children sent abroad be fully and publicly recognised.

Cottages homes – replicating the family?

From the 1870s on 'cottage homes' were an attempt by both voluntary organisations and Poor Law unions alike to create smaller scale institutions, closer to family life. Typically, the units, perhaps eight or ten in number, were divided by gender and between Protestants and Catholics, with each cottage housing two dozen children in three bedrooms.

Children's wellbeing depended on the personality and energy of the woman in charge of each cottage who was rarely off duty. She 'cooks, repairs clothing, sends the children to school and gives them what training is possible after school hours', as a conference in 1906 was told (14). The Labour MP for Woolwich, Will Crooks, who favoured removing children from the Poor Law altogether, commented (15):

> 'It was claimed for these cottages…that they are like workmen's homes, but [I] had never seen a workman's home in which there were sixteen children under fourteen years of age and one woman to look after them.'

'Scattered homes' took the attempt to replicate family life a step further: individual houses in residential districts each with eight or nine rooms, the forerunner of the local authority 'family group homes'. Sheffield Union, among the first to develop them, ran nine homes with between 15 and 28 beds. Each house was presided over by a foster mother, assisted by older children, and like children in cottage homes, they attended the local primary school in everyday clothing. The local press considered the system a success because they taught the values of the respectable working class. Will Crooks was still not convinced (16):

> 'There was a time when everybody went mad over this reform, when everybody said, "What you want is a scattered home with a mother in it". It was thought then that mothers could be got like dock labourers …'

The long legacy of the 19th century

Evangelical organisations and Poor Law unions learned from each other despite having different moral and organisational cultures. Visiting Poor Law officials praised Stephenson's National Children's Home on Bonner Road in London while unions increasingly paid for places in voluntary homes because it was cheaper to board than to build new homes (17).

Some historians have argued that workhouses and district schools were a 'disciplinary space' enacted on the bodies of the children (18). Such arguments need be balanced with a fuller understanding of the day-to-day care. That both Poor Law and voluntary care aimed to train children to find work as part of the respectable working class, however, is indisputable.

Children in Care 1900-1914, England and Wales (approximate numbers)

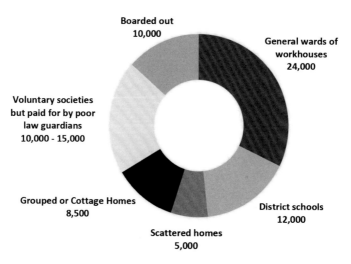

Boarded out
10,000

General wards of workhouses
24,000

Voluntary societies but paid for by poor law guardians
10,000 - 15,000

Grouped or Cottage Homes
8,500

District schools
12,000

Scattered homes
5,000

Adapted from *H. Hendrick Child Welfare Historical dimensions, contemporary debate* Bristol: Policy Press, 2003 p.42

The First World War and subsequent years of austerity effectively shut down further reform. Public care of children became frozen in time. True, local authorities took over responsibilities for workhouses, children's homes and boarding out from the Poor Law unions in 1930, but this was, essentially, an administrative reform. Poor Law attitudes and staff remained in place as workhouses were converted into children's homes under new public assistance departments, while boarding out placements and their supervision remained reliant on mostly untrained voluntary visitors working to three different local authority committees.

Drift also occurred in the voluntary sector. William Quarrier's vast conglomerate of homes continued to be managed by his family decades after the founder's death in 1903. In the 1920s, Barnardo's staff served 20 years on average, while careers of 30 to 40 years were not unusual. Senior managers remained in place for many years, with two members of the general council in 1943 having been appointed when Barnardo, who died in 1905, was still alive (19). There was no formal training for Barnardo's staff until 1941 when child psychology was introduced for the first time (even later for the Church of England Waifs and Strays Society, now the Children's Society).

Children's emotional life remained a largely closed book. Not until the late 1940s did staff realise that parents, as Eileen Younghusband put it, 'lived on inside the child' and that the child's emotional life had also to be nurtured along with food and shelter (20).

A new start?

The Second World War from 1939–45 prompted an overdue appraisal of children in care. Evacuation from working class urban districts had revealed differences in class attitudes toward hygiene and parental control as complaints from middle class families with whom children were billeted came pouring in. A talented group of child psychoanalysts delved more closely into the effects of separation for children abruptly removed from home, among them John Bowlby and Susan Isaacs, who studied evacuees in Cambridge, and Anna Freud, who studied children in residential nurseries (21). Until this point, a child's need for a steady, reliable, nurturing attachment had gone unnoticed.

The war experience exposed the ramshackle, piecemeal arrangements for children in public care administered by multiple local authority departments with different regulations. Two investigative committees appointed by government – the Clyde Committee in Scotland on homeless children, and the Curtis Committee on children in care in England and Wales – developed broadly similar recommendations. In England, the Committee found 19th century institutions on depressing display, including workhouses used for the intake of very young children (22), and overcrowded cottage homes that were far from 'anything that resembles an actual family group' (23). The report built the case for foster rather than residential care as the first choice for most children. By contrast, the Clyde Committee saw a positive, specialist role for residential care in a country that had long favoured fostering; it further recommended ending all crofter foster placements (24). Foster care in both countries was administered by multiple local authority departments with visits to placements by untrained volunteers. Both reports recommended placing all aspects of children in public care in the hands of a new single local authority department. These were duly created by the Children Act of 1948 with a duty to work toward returning a child received into care to its family.

The new departments notwithstanding, change came slowly, reflected in substandard accommodation and high caseloads among field staff.

In the mid-1960s childcare officers were *still* placing children in working boys hostels, receiving homes, residential nurseries, cottage homes, large voluntary children's homes, mother and baby hostels (created by voluntary moral welfare societies but now mainly under local authorities), special schools and hospitals for children with disabilities (25). Residential care continued to practise by rule of thumb, following what the largely untrained staff thought was best for children. Only rudimentary information was available on individual children coming into care, and none at all on the age and gender of children in care as a whole or what kinds of care was the most effective. Knowledge of child development on the ground was scant, and particular difficulties, such as autism and hyperactivity, were unknown territory (26).

But substantial change finally got underway, first in Scotland in the mid-1960s when the Kilbrandon Report (27) recommended young offenders be dealt with by a lay panel enabled to discuss the offence and matters of upbringing with parents and child. These children's hearings (as they were termed), outside the criminal justice system, became a central means for reforming Scottish children's services through the Social Work (Scotland) Act of 1968 (28). It became the point of divergence with England and Wales where criminal prosecution of children remained widely practised.

In England and Wales new local authority departments were created in 1971 following recommendations of the Seebohm Committee, bringing social services for children and adults under one roof. They were soon challenged when the death of a child, Maria Colwell in Brighton in 1973, pointed to lapses in supervision of children in care. By the mid-1970s new advocates for family support argued forcefully that poverty, especially among lone-parent families, was often the central but unspoken reason why children came into care (29).

The limits of the local authority as 'corporate parent' became apparent. Children waited too long for placements and those in care lost contact with family and were below average in educational attainment (30). The ubiquitous local authority family group home (31)

> 'can never be 'a family'; …the term "family group" now describes the staffing structure of these establishments, rather than perceptions of the children's residential experience.'

The abusive Frank Beck in Leicester and the Pindown regime in Staffordshire showed that some homes had become self-governing fiefdoms that senior managers had turned a blind eye to (32).

The poet Lemn Sissay's memoir of his time in care captures the unpredictability of the system in 1980 when he was 12 (33):

> 'Children were moved haphazardly from home to home as objects of low emotional currency. Damaged goods. It was nothing personal. You had to have your wits about you to hold on to anything. Money, lighters, socks, bracelets, biros, cigarettes, all of it needed secure hiding places: under floorboards, holes in brickwork under a windowsill.'

His local authority records show how social workers, foster parents and children home staff rationalised their high-handed and often racist actions even when apparently consulting him, revealing widespread attitudes in the years before social services departments began to tackle discrimination against minority ethnic groups.

Local authority homes had come to serve four main functions: emergency admissions; children waiting for foster placements or for whom placements had failed; adolescents with strong family ties; and 'long term casualties' of the care system (34). Keeping siblings together improved the chance of a successful placement, as did frequent contact with parents, while children placed with relatives ('kinship care' as it came to be called) were twice as stable as stranger fostering (35). The Kent Family Placement Project was the first to better prepare foster carers for work with children on short-term placements, buttressed by better assessments of children's behaviour and higher levels of support – beginning a decisive trend in both training and tasks that foster carers were asked to take on.

Voluntary organisations embarked on a period of sustained innovation as they closed their residential homes from the 1970s on. The range of NCH projects – mediation, intermediate treatment and youth justice, family counselling, support for families with learning disability – is indicative of its transformation (36). Barnardo's shifted its focus to families in need, children with disabilities, and family centres, overthrowing the rescue philosophy of its origin (37). Knowledge of difficult behaviour and how it was experienced by the child also improved. Not until the 1980s, for example, did the social and perceptual difficulties of autism start to be better understood, as parents and support groups began to describe their experiences of raising an autistic child (38). Whether formally therapeutic or not, it became widely understood that residential care sought to modify behaviour through social interaction and nurturing, 'allowing children to develop, learn gain self–confidence, mature emotionally' (39). New regulations issued in the wake of the Children Act 1989 underscored residential care as part of an overall network of services with staff central to the involvement of children in decision-making, and planning and reviews, and making the increased contact under the Act a success (40).

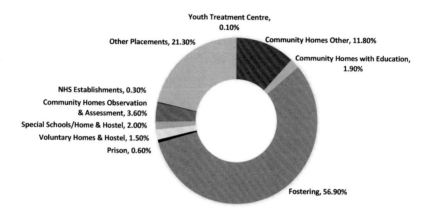

Children in Care 1990, England
Total number: 60,469

W. Utting *Children in the Public Care A Review of Residential Child Care*, HMSO, 1991, p.27.

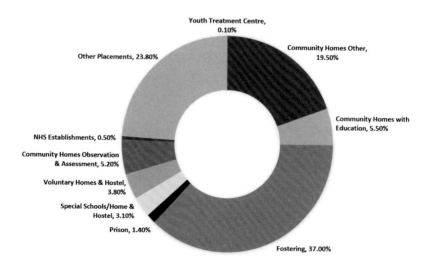

Children in Care 1980, England
Total number: 95,297

W. Utting *Children in the Public Care A Review of Residential Child Care*, HMSO, 1991, p.27.

The new millennium

Following the enquiry into the death of Victoria Climbié in 2001 while under local authority supervision, children's services were once again separated from adult services (41). The death of another child, Peter Connelly, in 2007 exerted immense public and political pressure on local authorities to prioritise child protection. The consequence was an historic 70 per cent increase in care applications between 2008–9 and 2012–13 and a 64 per cent increase in referrals per 10,000 children (42). From then on, safeguarding effectively overwhelmed family support as the core of practice.

Under the NHS and Community Care Act 1991 local authorities were encouraged to see themselves as 'enabling' rather than providing services. Cautiously at first and then rapidly, they closed their children's homes, in thrall to the idea that 'quasi-markets' would exert cost discipline on their budgets but still remain under their control (43). In this they were mistaken. As quasi-markets became actual markets, public provision was privatised by degrees. By 2020 commercial companies provided 70 per cent of residential care places in England, in Wales, 78 per cent (44).

A similar trend happened in fostering. The Care Standards Act 2000 permitted local authorities to use independent fostering agencies (IFAs) to supplement their own provision with different options and skills but it was not long before IFAs became part of the mainstream service as local authorities struggled to provide placements in sufficient number. As a consequence, children are often placed at distance from their home authority, vulnerable to exploitation and abuse (45) while private providers extract higher profits from local authorities forced to buy places urgently on the 'spot market'. They simply do not have the purchasing clout to reshape 'a fragmented, uncoordinated and irrational market that ultimately does not meet the needs of children' (46). In Scotland, with greater governmental scepticism of the role of markets, 35 per cent of children were in for-profit homes in 2020 while for-profit foster agencies were banned altogether.

The Promise programme in Scotland, acknowledges that the interconnections between poverty and the care system are so profound that 'there must be significant and persistent commitment' to eradicating it (47). Residential care is for those children on whom social and familial stress has taken its toll and who find the intensity of foster families overwhelming. The work is therapeutic, rights–based and trauma-informed, with staff recruited for their values rather than their education (48). The future of children's residential and foster care will be shaped by how well these principles hold their own in the years to come.

What does the future hold? It is certain that residential and foster care will remain integral to children's services. Voluntary organisations are committed to therapeutic approaches dealing with children's trauma across the UK, meeting a national crisis in adolescent mental health.

References

(1)   Mouat, F., 'On the education and training of the children of the poor', *Journal of the Statistical Society of London*, 43 (2) 187, 1880.

(2)   Shaw, C., *When I was a Child*, London: Caliban Books, pp. 96–7, 1903/1977.

(3)   National Archives, Home Office-73-53-11. Answer to circular of the 28 July 1837 no. 79.

(4)   Hodgkinson, R., *The Origins of the National Health Service the Medical Services of the New Poor Law 1834–1871*, London: Wellcome Historical Medical Library, pp. 550–1, 1967.

(5)   Cree, V., 'History of Social Work in Scotland'. In V. Cree and M. Smith (Eds) *Social Work in Scotland*. Abingdon: Routledge, p. 14, 2018.

(6)   Abrams, L., *The Orphan Country Children of Scotland's Broken Homes From 1845 to the Present Day*. Edinburgh: John Donald, p. 11, 1998.

(7)   Mason, M., quoted in Chance, W., *Children Under the Poor Law*. London: Swan Sonnenschein and Co., pp. 391–2, 1897.

(8)   quoted in Chance, W., as above, p. 193.

(9)   For the enemies that this approach created see Wagner, Gillian, Barnardo. London: Weidenfeld and Nicolson, p. 46, 1979.

(10) Philpot, T., *Action for Children*. Oxford: Lion, p. 21, 1994.

(11) Parr, J., *Labouring Children: British Immigrant Apprentices to Canada, 1869–1924*. London: Croom Helm, p. 159, 1980.

(12) Gammie, A. (not dated) *William Quarrier and the Story of the Orphan Homes of Scotland*. Edinburgh: Pickering and Inglis, pp. 88–9.

(13) Doyle, A., *Emigration of Pauper Children to Canada Local Government Board 1875*, p. 29.

(14) Poor Law Conferences 1905–6, South-Western District Conference 1906. London: P.S. King, pp. 469–71, 1906.

(15) *Yorkshire Post and Leeds Intelligencer* Friday 18 June 1909.

(16) 'Children in Workhouses', *London Daily News*, 4 August 1911.

(17) Philpot, T., *Action for Children*. Oxford: Lion, p. 30, 1994.

(18) See, for example, Driver, F., *Power and Pauperism: The Workhouse System 1834–1884*. Cambridge: Cambridge University Press, 1993.

(19) Hitchman, J., *They Carried the Sword. The Barnardo Story*. London: Gollancz, p. 15, 1966.

(20) Younghusband, E., *Social Work in Britain 1950–1975: A Follow-up Study: Volume 1*, London: George Allen and Unwin, p. 36, 1978.

(21) Isaacs, S. (Ed) *The Cambridge Evacuation Survey*. London: Methuen and Co., 1941; Burlingham, D. and Freud, A., *Young Children in War Time: A Year's Work in a Residential Nursery*. London: George Allen and Unwin Ltd, 1944.

(22) Curtis, M., *Report of the Care of Children*. London: HMSO, para 136, 1946.

(23) Curtis (as above), paras 16; 261; 267.

(24) Clyde, J., *Report of the Committee on Homeless Children*. Edinburgh: HMSO, 1946.

(25) Stroud, J., *Childcare Officers and Their World*. London: Victor Gollancz, 1965.

(26) Bullock, R., 'Childcare past and present', *The Therapeutic Care Journal*, 1 April, 2008.

(27) Asquith, S. (Ed) The Kilbrandon Report. Scotland: HMSO, 1964. Available online, with updates and reflection at: https://www.gov.scot/publications/kilbrandon-report/pages/3/

(28) Children and Young Persons, Scotland: Report of the Committee Edinburgh: HMSO, 1964.

(29) See, for example, Holman, B., *Inequality in Childcare*. London: Child Poverty Action Group, 1976.

(30) Rowe, J. and Lambert, L. *Children Who Wait*. London: British Agencies for Adoption and Fostering, 1975; Milham, S. *et al*, *Lost in Care*. Aldershot: Gower Publishing, 1986; Jackson, S., *Education of Children in Care*. Bristol: University of Bristol, 1988; Family Rights Group, *Promoting Links: Keeping children and families in touch*. London: FRG, 1976.

(31) Berridge, David, quoted in Utting, W., *Children in the Public Care: A Review of Residential Childcare*. London: HMSO, p. 31, 1991.

(32) Levy, A. and Kahan, B., *The Pindown Experience and the Protection of Children*. Staffordshire County Council, 1991.

(33) Sissay, L., *My Name Is Why*. Edinburgh: Canongate, p. 93, 2019.

(34) Utting, W., *Children in the Public Care: A Review of Residential Childcare*. London: HMSO, p. 31, 1991.

(35) Berridge, D. and Cleaver, H., *Foster Home Breakdown*. Oxford: Blackwell, pp. 182–2, 1987.

(36) Philpot, T., *Action for Children*. Oxford: Lion, Chapter 9, 1994.

(37) See, for example, Jack, G. and Gill, O., *The Missing Side of the of the Triangle: Assessing the Importance of Family and Environment Factors in the Lives of Children*. Barkingside: Barnardos, 2003.

(38) Wolff, S., 'The history of autism', *European Child and Adolescent Psychiatry*, 13 (4) 201–208, 2004.

(39) Parker, R., *Residential Care: The Research Reviewed: Children*. London: Department of Health, p. 107–8, 1988.

(40) Department of Health, *The Children Act 1989. Guidance and Regulations Volume 4 Residential Care*. London: HMSO, pp. 1 and 69, 1991.

(41) Laming, L., *The Victoria Climbie Inquiry: Report of an inquiry by Lord Laming*. London: The Stationery Office, 2003. https://www.gov.uk/government/publications/the-victoria-climbie-inquiry-report-of-an-inquiry-by-lord-laming

(42) Pemberton, C., 'Care applications rise 70% in years since Baby P Case', *Community Care* May 9, 2013. https://www.communitycare.co.uk/2013/05/09/care-applications-rise-70-in-years-since-baby-p-case/

(43) Pierson, J., *A New History of Social Work Values and Practice in the Struggle for Social Justice*. Abingdon: Routledge, pp. 186–7, 2002.

(44) Children's Commissioner for England, *Private Provision in Children's Social Care*. London: CCE, p. 4, 2020.

(45) Children's Commissioner for England, *Private Provision in Children's Social Care*. London: CCE, 2020.

(46) Competition and Markets Authority, *Children's Social Care Market Study*. Interim Report. London: CMA, 2021.

(47) 'The Promise'. *Independent Care Review,* p. 18. https://www.carereview.scot/wp-content/uploads/2020/02/The-Promise.pdf

(48) The Promise, as above, p. 79.

loyal

fun

Funny

I WILL SUCCEED

optimistic

brave

I can succeed

Giving Children a Voice

Creative projects are regularly commissioned for the children by Five Rivers Child Care: here they describe their feelings while being in care.

I can dream

open-minded

empathetic

I CAN DREAM

I am a star

energetic

kind-hearted

CHAPTER 2

Why Residential Care?

Ann Buchanan

Introduction

A key principle of the Children Act 1989 is that children are best looked after within their families, with their parents playing a full part in their lives. But sometimes children cannot be safely cared for by their parents and state intervention is necessary to protect and promote their welfare (1).

This chapter explores the number of children who are looked after; government requirements and expectations for children in their care; outcomes for children from different types of placements; and the different types of problems they present (mental health, substance misuse and criminality). It outlines issues in providing residential care, different types of residential settings, the challenges presented by young people in these settings and, finally, explores how we may do better.

Who are the children in the social care system in England?

Out of the 12 million children living in England in 2020/2021, just under 400,000 (three per cent) are in the social care system at any one time. Most of these children are able to live at home with support and supervision. However, 80,850 children of these children were not able to live at home and were looked-after children or children in state care. This figure, which has continued to rise in recent years, is at an all-time high (2).

In 2020/21, nearly three quarters of all children in care were fostered (3). A quarter of these were in the care of family and friends (kinship care) and the remainder in non-family households, including a range of children's homes and residential care. Just under 3,000 were adopted. In Narey's report on residential care in England in 2016, he notes that as of 31 March 2015, 8,320 children were in residential care. Of these, 5,290 were in children's homes, 60 in residential schools, 180 in secure units and 110 in hostels (4).

Government policy in England for looked-after children

Children Act 1989, Regulations and Guidance Volume 2 outlines how looked-after children should be care for state (5):

> 'Looked-after children deserve the best experiences in life, from excellent parenting which promotes good health and educational attainment, to a wide range of opportunities to develop their talents and skills in order to have an enjoyable childhood and successful adult life. Stable placements, good health and support during transition are all essential elements, but children will only achieve their potential through the ambition and high expectation of all those involved in their lives.'

A key principle in planning the care and future of looked after children is the concept of 'permanence'.

Permanence is the long-term plan for the child's upbringing and provides an underpinning framework for all social work with children and their families from family support through to adoption. The objective of planning for permanence is therefore to ensure that children have a secure, stable and loving family to support them through childhood and beyond and to give them a sense of security, continuity, commitment, identity and belonging. One of the key functions of the care plan is to ensure that each child has a plan for permanence.

Achieving permanence for a child will be a key consideration from the day the child becomes looked-after. The permanence planning process, informed by multi-agency contributions, will identify which permanence option is most likely to meet the needs of the individual child, taking account of his/her wishes and feelings.

A range of options for permanence exist, all of which can deliver good outcomes for individual children (6):

> 'For many children, permanence is achieved through a successful return to their birth family, where it has been possible to address the factors in family life which led to the child becoming looked-after. For other children routes to permanence outside the care system may include: family and friends care, particularly where such care can be supported by a legal order such as a child arrangement order, special guardianship order or in a few cases, adoption; adoption, which for many children can offer the best route to a lifelong and legally permanent new family.'

The first challenge: How to achieve this?

In 2008 the Department of Health commissioned a review on the factors associated with outcomes for looked-after children (7). Ninety-two studies were included: four systematic reviews, five non–systematic reviews, eight randomised controlled trials, sixty-six cohort studies, and nine cross-sectional studies. From the review, there appeared to be some key factors that were associated with a range of outcomes, in particular, number of placements, behavioural problems and age at first placement. Placement instability and behavioural problems appeared to be central to less positive outcomes.

Lack of placement stability is a problem for child welfare agencies across the world. In the US, a report from the Casey Foundation, *Placement Stability Strategies – Casey Family Programs* (8) found that the most stable placements, after adoption, were those with family and kin, but children with behavioural problems were strongly associated with placement instability.

Increase in behavioural problems amongst children in general

The dilemma is that rates of mental disorders in children have increased since 2017. In 2020 one in six (16 per cent) children aged five to sixteen years were identified as having a probable mental disorder, increasing from one in nine (10.8 per cent) in 2017. The likelihood of a probable mental disorder increased with age with a noticeable difference in gender for the older age group (17 to 22 years); 27.2 per cent of young women and 13.3 per cent of young men were identified as having a probable mental disorder (9).

Impact of Covid

More than half of young people aged between 11 and 22 said that lockdown had made their life worse. Linked to this are the problems their parents experience during lockdown. Children aged 5 to 16 years with a probable mental disorder were more than twice as likely to live in a household that had fallen behind with payments than children unlikely to have a mental disorder. Among 11 to 16-year-old girls, nearly two-thirds with a probable mental disorder, had seen or heard an argument among adults in their household, compared to less than half of those unlikely to have a mental disorder (9). When it came to children who were looked after, government statistics in 2021 showed that more than two-thirds of young people had behavioural problems that were a cause for concern.

Substance misuse

A significant proportion of young people with mental health needs, also have a problem with substance misuse. Nearly 15,000 young people were in contact with alcohol and drug services between April 19 and March 2020 (10).

Young people involved with specialist substance misuse services come with a range of problems or vulnerabilities associated with (or in addition to) their substance use. These include using multiple different substances, not being in education, employment or training, and being a looked-after child. Other wider risk factors can also impact on their substance use, such as self-harming behaviour, sexual exploitation, offending or domestic abuse.

Youth Justice

The Laming Report in 2015 suggests between six per cent and eight per cent of looked-after children enter the youth justice system. While this figure implies that most children in care will not enter the youth justice system, it is nevertheless double the three per cent of children, from the general population, who offend. Multiple placement breakdown and moves are often cited as a reason for instability which is linked to an increased likelihood of offending (11).

Who are the children in residential care?

Children who are looked after may be suffering from the experiences before they came into care. These experiences may have had a negative impact of their emotional development and be reflected in their behaviour in his or her placement, in schools and other aspects of his or her life. Emotional and behavioural difficulties may have been the trigger for entering care in the first place. New evidence from neuroscience provides clear evidence on the link between early abuse and neglect and brain development including the development of social and emotional skills (12). But it is also important to remember that looked-after children can be further disturbed by the care they receive after becoming looked after. Reports from young people in care can paint a grim picture of the challenges they have faced, including frequent changes of placement, schools, social workers and disrupted friendships and worse (13).

Shaw found that, of the looked-after children who were in residential homes and/or the youth justice system in 2014, those who lived in residential care were inevitably the most challenging children and their pre-care experiences, including abuse, neglect and poor parenting and multiple placement moves had played a part in entering the care system (14).

A systematic review in 2015 (15) found that children were often placed in residential care once other placement options, such as foster care, had been unsuccessful. Only a quarter had a children's home as their first placement. Therefore, children living in children's homes had often experienced multiple previous placements and carers. Children living in residential care were more likely than other looked-after children to have poor mental health (nearly three-quarters, according to one study). This suggests that the majority of children living in residential care in England are likely to have some therapeutic needs.

Richman (16) has noted that when children were extremely distressed, traditional psychiatric therapies were initially of little use. The first challenge with such children was to 'normalise' the child's life, to settle them in school, and into a routine. With some of the extremely distressed children entering care, residential care may offer them the necessary security to settle their behaviour.

However, it would be wrong to characterise residential care as only for the very disturbed. Some looked-after children choose to go to a children's home rather than to be fostered, as noted by a young man who spoke to Narey in his report of residential care (17):

> 'Younger children are better in foster placements because it's important for them to have a family. As I was older, I felt I already had a family and didn't want a new one.'

Types of residential care

Looked-after children in residential care may be placed in a variety of settings. The following map shows the number and types of different residential settings for children and the changes between March 2020 and March 2021.

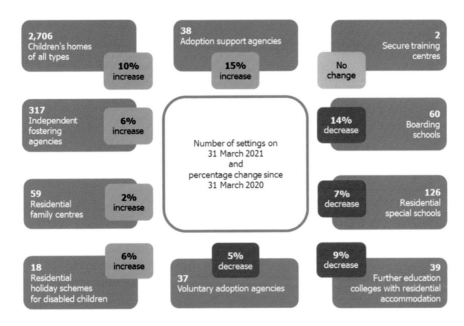

Figure 1: The number of settings as at 31 March 2021 by provider type, and the change from 31 March 2020 (18)

In 2016, the Narey report (19) notes that the voluntary sector provided relatively little residential care; only about five per cent of children were in homes provided by the voluntary sector; over a quarter of children lived in local authority provision, while the majority of children, lived in privately-run provisions. In 2015, the average weekly cost of a place in a children's home was approximately £3,000, and there was little difference in cost between local authority, voluntary sector and private sector provision. There were more staff in local authority homes and they were generally paid more. Staff in privately run homes worked longer hours. Although Narey welcomed the dramatic shift in recent decades to greater use of fostering (particularly specialist fostering for more demanding young people), he felt there was a very real and unmet demand for greater use of children's homes and that it would not be in children's interests to reduce our reliance of their use.

He was sceptical about the need for a child always to be placed near home as he felt with modern media, Zoom and other tools, contact could now be maintained with their family from afar. The quality of the care was, he felt, more important than the distance.

He also worried that some residential placements were ended too early. Because of the cost, local authorities may be tempted to return a young person to home or fostering too soon. Moving a child who was happy in a school, and whose behaviour had settled, risked a repeat of earlier disturbances. Some longer-term placements in children's homes achieved very good outcomes. As one of the young men he interviewed said (20):

> 'Residential care was my home; it was my life and it is still a big memory… Residential care absolutely turned my life around and I now am in a position where I am studying social work and giving back to the community… This would not have happened should I have remained in foster care.'

How can we do better for children in residential care?

Do we need to know more?

Inevitably, the quick answer is 'yes'. The Narey report notes some high-quality care, particularly care that avoided further criminalisation of young people taking place, but we need more research on 'What works?' or 'What works best?'. The government's What Works Centre for Children's Social Care provides an excellent opportunity for encouraging a stronger and urgently needed evidence base for the best children's residential care (21). A report from the What Works Centre for Children's Social Care was publishing a report on Children Living in Residential Care in April 2022, too late to be detailed in this chapter but it does say (22):

> 'This analysis aims to provide a quantitative national overview of the characteristics and experiences of children living in residential care, their journeys into and out of residential care placements and their outcomes compared to children in other types of care.'

In the short-term, residential care is an expensive option, but if it manages to turn some young people's lives around, it will be a considerable saving over the life course (fewer mental health problems, less dependency on welfare, and so on).

Do we need to take a longer-term perspective about care and support?

My view, based on practice and over 30 years of research, is that currently, under the Children Act 1989, although young people leaving care are entitled to some further support from the public parent, 'permanence' is still a temporary concept, lasting only until the young person has left care. Should we think about outcomes in the longer term? My own research, *What Happened When They Were Grown Up*, using the data from the National Children Development Study, tracked children over 33 years, that is, children born in 1958. Adult outcomes for children who had been in care were dismal compared to those, even the extremely disadvantaged, who remained at home (23). Undoubtedly, things have improved since then. But currently, under the Children Act 1989, 'permanence' seems to mean until a young person leaves care or is no longer supported after leaving further education.

More recently, I undertook a study of elders, aged 70, 80 and 90, who had been in Barnardo's care since early childhood (24). These elders had been taken from their families after the war and came from extremely desperate situations. Although some elders had bad experiences, as since has been discovered in the residential care system (25), many spoke very positively about their life under Barnardo's and on leaving care, the long-term stability they had achieved while in care enabled many to lead important and useful lives. It was impressive to hear how Barnardo's viewed their responsibilities. They gave young people who had been in their care real skills that enabled them to obtain work, and helped them find lodgings. Some in early adulthood, when faced with a crisis (for instance with an unexpected pregnancy), were able to return and receive further assistance. It struck me that Barnardo's acted as most parents do while their young are negotiating their role in the world. Proverbially speaking, they 'stay with them'. Although young people leaving care have rights to ask for support from social services after they have left care, it is my impression this is fairly limited.

Do we need to help looked-after children keep contact with siblings?

In the above study, Barnardo's encouraged a clean break from their past and most rarely saw their parent or brothers and sisters unless they were placed together. Nowadays, this is very different and parents are consulted and encouraged to be involved at very stage. Again, my impression is that siblings are rarely involved. Siblings are, however, likely to be the longest lasting relationships a child has, much longer than their parents (26).

In my Barnardo's study, it was poignant that as older people, the Barnardo's elders went to enormous lengths to reconnect with their siblings. They apparently needed to do this to affirm their identity ('Who am I?'), but also to find family help and support from their siblings as they aged.

The message I took from this study is that long-term residential care can give stability to some young people who would otherwise have remained very disturbed, but at the same time it was important for those in residential are to retain contact with not only parents but possibly more importantly, with their siblings as these were the family who would look after them in later life.

References

(1) Department of Education, *Children Act 1989. Guidance and Regulations, Volume 2. Update 2021.* London: Department of Education, p. 9, 2021.

(2) Office for National Statistics, *Children Looked After in England Including Adoptions. Reporting Year 2021*. London: ONS, 2021.

(3) Office for National Statistics, *Children Looked After in England*. London: ONS, 2021. https://www.gov.uk/government/statistics/fostering–in–england–1–april–2020–to–31–march–2021/fostering–in–england–2020–to–2021–main–findings

(4) Narey, M., *Residential Care in England*. London: Government UK, 2016.

(5) Department of Education, as above (1)

(6) Department of Education, as above (1)

(7) Jones, R., Everson-Hock, E.S., Papaioannou, S. *et al*, 'Factors associated with outcomes for looked-after children and young people: A correlated review of the literature'. *Health Development*, 37 (5) 613–22, 2011.

(8) Casey Family Programs, *Placement Stability Strategies*. CFP, 2018. www.casey.org/strategies-improve-placement-stability

(9) NHS Digital, *Mental Health of Children and Young People in England, 2020: Wave 1*. (Follow up to the 2017 Survey). London: NHS, 2020.

(10) Government UK, *Young People's Substance Misuse Treatment Statistics 2019 to 2020: Report*. London: Government UK, 2020.

(11) Youth Justice Board, *Keeping Children in Care Out of Trouble: An Independent Review chaired by Lord Laming. Response by the Youth Justice Board for England and Wales to the Call for Views and Evidence August 2015.* London: Youth Justice Board, 2016.

(12) Department of Education, as above (1).

(13) Buchanan, A., 'Young people's views on being looked after in out-of-home-care under The Children Act 1989'. *Children and Youth Services Review*, 17 (5–6) 681–69, 1995.

(14) Shaw, J., *Residential Children's Homes and the Youth Justice System: Identity, Power and Perceptions*. London: Palgrave Macmillan, 2014.

(15) Strijbosch, E. L. L., Huijs, J. A. M., Stams, G. J. J. M. *et al*, 'The outcome of institutional youth care compared to non-institutional youth care for children of primary school age and early adolescence: A multi-level meta-analysis'. *Children and Youth Services Review*, 58, 208–218, 2015.

(16) Richman, N., *In the Midst of the Whirlwind. A Manual for Helping Refugee Children*. London: Trentham Books, 1998.

(17) Narey, M., as above (4).

(18) Ofsted, *Ofsted Main Findings: Children's Social Care in England 2021*. London: Ofsted, 2021.

(19) Narey, M., as above (4).

(20) Narey, M., p. 6, as above (4).

(21) What Works for Children's Social Care (whatworks-csc.org.uk), 2022.

(22) What Works for Children's Social Care, *Children Living in Residential Care*. London: What Works in Children's Social Care. (whatworks-csc.org.uk), 2022.

(23) Buchanan, A. and Ten Brinke, J., *What Happened When They Were Grown Up? Outcomes from Parenting Experiences*. York: York Publishing Service, 1997.

(24) Buchanan, A., 'Linking up again: Views of Barnardo's elders on being separated from their siblings and how they reconnected in old age'. In A. Buchanan and A. Rotkirch (Eds) *Brothers and Sisters: Sibling Relationships over the Life Course*. London: Palgrave Macmillan, 2021.

(25) Buchanan, A., 'Young people's views on being looked after in out-of-home-care under The Children Act 1989', *Children and Youth Services Review*, 17 (5–6) 681–696, 1995.

(26) Buchanan, A. and Rotkirch, A. (Eds), *Brothers and Sister: Sibling Relationships over the Life Course*. London: Palgrave Macmillan, 2021.

CHAPTER 3

Reversing the Impacts of Childhood Complex Trauma

Richard M. Cross

Introduction

This chapter aims to provide as much helpful and valuable information to those engaged in therapeutic care for children who have experienced complex trauma. Whether in therapeutic education, residential, foster care or, for that matter, involved in social work or the commissioning of services. What follows is an exploration of some *active ingredients* that can assist in understanding and providing relational-based recovery for traumatised children.

It reflects the understanding of Cozolino, who stated (1):

> 'Those who are nurtured best, survive best.'

It also seeks to highlight the need to move towards services for children that are trauma-responsive and aims to explore the whole question of what is 'therapeutic'. One key aspect of our work is to be able to 'acknowledge' and set clear expectations.

There are no speedy one-week interventions to undo the repeated harm caused by abusive caregivers. Care services, organisations and individuals need to embrace the emerging scientific understanding of 'what works' and offer the opportunity for children to have access to the right services when needed.

This text does not seek to cover all the bases. Still, it aims to provide a springboard to create curiosity and encourage the continued exploration of some highlighted areas. Above all, this suggests a range of opportunities to support practitioners in understanding and respond to the natural and normal survival responses that children may have developed. While keeping in the front of our minds not 'What is wrong with you?', but rather, 'What has happened to you?' (2).

Complex trauma

There are numerous definitions of complex trauma; children have often explained the repeated overwhelming traumatising experiences inflicted by primary carers or the extended family system. This often places the scene of the 'crime' within the home environment characterised by repeated experiences of fear without a solution.

There is an emerging understanding of the developmental impacts of overwhelming experiences on our bodies and minds. When these experiences are repetitive, our normal survival responses make it increasingly difficult to return to a place of safety in our bodies and the environment around us. For the first time, there is an acceptance that single event trauma, which can equally be debilitating, differs from experiences connected to repeated victimisation (3) during critical early development.

The following emphasises three strands of understanding which can offer the necessary understanding and awareness to work with complex trauma complexities: attachment, trauma, and dissociation.

1. Attachment

In his third volume of his Attachment and Loss (4), Bowlby writes:

> 'Intimate attachments to other human beings are the hub around which a person's life revolves, not only when he is an infant or toddler or a schoolchild but throughout his adolescence and his years of maturity as well, on to old age.'

In that trilogy Bowlby (4,5,6) identified that we are born with the inherent capacity for making emotional bonds, for instance, becoming attached to those who care for us in our childhood.

In his work, he identified two distinct sets of stimuli, separation and loss of / or from the caregiver. These experiences can elicit fear in the infant. They can lead them to steer towards seeking proximity to the caregiver as this is needed for survival. This activation from the 'fear' response is biological. It initiates the infant to seek to attach, regardless of whether the parent is caring or hurtful.

Attachment is a theory of 'relationships', not about the provision of labels, and is built upon three key concepts, which have at its core the notion of a 'secure base'. This is the creation of felt knowing within the child or adolescent that they can go out and explore the world with the knowledge that when they return, they will be welcomed and 'nourished physically and emotionally, comforted if distressed, reassured if frightened' (7).

- *Proximity seeking*: for survival reasons, a child needs the physical closeness of others.

- *Proximity maintaining*: the child will attach to those they are familiar with, whether they are nurturing or not.

- *Proximity promoting*: we adapt to optimise our proximity and survival (physical and psychological).

Early attachment is studied and assessed through a procedure developed by Mary Ainsworth (8). Two brief separations from a caregiver are observed, followed by two reunions with the carer. From this research, three patterns of organised behaviour were identified in infants who were around 18 months of age:

- *Secure*: the infant cries at separation and is quickly comforted at the reunion, empathically attuned response

- *Insecure avoidant*: the infant does not cry at separation and actively avoids the caregiver during the reunion

- *Insecure-ambivalent*: the infant cries at separation but is not easily comforted on the reunion.

Some infants who could not organise attachment behaviour according to any unitary or coherent pattern were classified as having a disorganised/disorientated pattern of attachment (9, 10). This pattern develops out of a relationship within which the parent is frightened of or frightening to the child. As Heijer reminds us (11):

> 'When a flower doesn't bloom, you fix the environment in which it grows, not the flower.'

Despite relationships being the source of so much hurt and pain, they can also have the power to ensure healing. What follows is a template for this therapeutic relational journey.

2. Trauma and adversity

Bowlby made a unique contribution in emphasising the experiences of children and moving away from what at that time was a focus on the importance of 'fantasy' and instead focusing and keeping in mind the actual real-life experiences of the children.

He asserted that children who did not receive empathic care (12) could have significant impacts on them, such as presenting difficulties, which was referred to back in time as 'delinquency'. He was also one of the first to emphasise the impacts of childhood adversity, which was novel at the time, highlighting that the children's emotional trauma 'mean far more to children than most grown-ups conceive possible' (6).

Today, there is a significant focus on the impacts of the adverse childhood experiences (13) and the acknowledgement that children who are looked after (14) are disproportionality exposed to events which may create toxic stressful situations.

Our bodies have evolved to be highly responsive and adaptive. We are designed for survival, and our reactions to 'fear and threat' ensure we can respond in the blink of an eye without conscious thought by releasing a fiery cocktail of hormones. In an instant, our bodies prepare for fight, flight or freeze. We have evolved to survive.

In the same way, all practitioners and carers need to be aware of our past painful experiences, what makes our bodies more likely to become dysregulated and be open to working on these areas in supervision and using approaches to 'recognise, acknowledge and calm' these physiological responses, to return to our best selves so we can remain in a position of empathic connectedness with the child.

When we are our best selves, we can be relational, empathise, engage, and have all our thinking resources at our disposal. Any human being (infant, child, and adult) can experience situations which move us out of this regulated state (affect). In these situations, we are not feeling safe, and our reflective capacity is reduced. It is critical to have the necessary knowledge to psycho-educate children – that is, to help them understand what is happening in their bodies and minds.

Moving from different affective states and regaining regulation is a crucial element of good mental health; it is a natural and normal response to moving between states through our ups and downs throughout life. Life is not pain-free; we can all experience distress.

The challenge becomes when this response which is part of our autonomic nervous system (ANS), becomes sensitised or stuck on. Our bodies are primed to support us in not experiencing any more painful experiences and seek to predict and identify threats. For this reason, 'avoidance' is critical in trauma symptoms, reminders, thoughts and stimuli associated with traumatic experiences. Anything that is detected can trigger a fear response.

A significant emphasis so far has been placed on the 'fear' response and how, as infants, we are hard-wired for attachment to improve our chances of survival. Similarly, our reactions to experiences which create traumatic 'fear or threat' activate our nervous systems (unconsciously), again creating within us a need to perform an 'action' such as running away or fighting; however, in many situations, the child's body is not able to respond as it would instinctually wish to do (that is, non-completion of action).

One of the core experiences of trauma is disconnection from others. Even though the child might be within an environment filled with adult figures, they may be on a desert island alone without access to anyone who can predictably provide care and protection (that is, the secure base).

For children who did not have the opportunity to internalise enough of the 'good stuff', therapeutic care can help reshape emotions and slowly allow the nervous systems to calm and not feel overwhelmed (16).

This is the *first* active ingredient required to take place between the adult and the child. The ability to 'transfer' (that is, in the psychological sense of transference) to the child the felt sense and understanding of how to return to a regulated state after being either hyper-aroused (fight or flight) or hypo-aroused (freeze, depressed, dissociation) state.

This 'calming' takes time and patience; we harness our understanding that nervous systems do not quickly switch off the response designed for protection. However, the plasticity of these systems means that change can occur through gentle and consistent recalibrating through the provided experience and transfer of the adult's affective regulatory capacities to the child or adolescent.

It is often illuminating that the children's nervous system responses are acting far more quickly than their 'thinking mind' can work. Therefore, when we experience a child's dysregulated affect and associated behaviours, it can appear that the trigger has been unseen. Let me give an example*:

> ### Example 1
>
> 'Get away from me!', she shouted, the sound carrying like a lightning bolt piercing the silence, almost making the air feel electrified all around her. It was her third day in care. She would not allow carers to support her no matter how hard they tried. She was terrified, lashing out as though she had to protect herself from something menacing and evil. It was disorientating; despite her being a small child, it felt like an adult was yelling at us, a presence in the room from the past. The carers needed something to help ground them, an understanding of what was happening between them and the child.

Affect is transmitted from body to body, which can mean the child's fear or terror can be transferred to us as the carer. If we understand what is happening, this can be a source of helpful knowledge; if not, this can become disorientating and activating for the adult nervous system. A child might be frightened, and as the carer, we may start to experience being frightened as well, as there is a transference of the fear from the child to us. It is important to emphasise this, as it is often the emotions and feelings within the adult caring system that create the dynamic of disconnection, which, sadly, can lead to placements ending.

In these moments, we must deploy our developed strategies if we either move towards hyper-arousal or hypo-arousal. Our safety plan is to reground and support ourselves to regain regulation and integration, so we are back within our window of tolerance. When skilled in using these strategies, we can bring these into the space between the child and us. It provides a direct source of helpfulness to the child through modeling and giving an experience of this, for example, practising our strategies, such as breathing calmly, ground strategies and other aspects of our personal 'regulation and resiliency' plan.

3. Dissociation

In situations of threat or fear, another adaptive option is to employ freezing, becoming non-acting; this is often experienced by a child who may become in a state of complete collapse.

In the animal kingdom, predators lose interest and stop attacking when they believe something is dead. This freeze response is called dissociation and is often described to me as 'being there but not there'. It is almost a magical ability to disconnect from thoughts, feelings, a sense of identity, and memories to create a disconnection. Often, children will describe feeling that they do not remember or that they experienced disconnecting from their body and floating above themselves, looking down at the unfolding traumatic experience, or having sudden rapid changes in mood. Again, an illustration:

> *Example 2*
>
> Everything was fun and there was lots of laughter at the table during dinner. Then suddenly it was like a tsunami washing through the kitchen, we all had to take cover, everything was suddenly being thrown around, then as soon as it had started there was stillness. The child was curled up in a ball rocking, seeking to access some form of comfort, I slowly moved towards the child to offer soothing and comfort. We found out later that mealtimes were experienced like a war zone for the child.

There is a need to be aware of this understanding alongside attachment and trauma to fully understand and make sense of how the child's developmental experiences have impacted them.

Above all, the very systems designed to provide care should be wary, not to dissociate or turn away from acknowledging the painful experiences that children have experienced.

Putting the pieces together

Trauma is stored as sensory experiences. When activated, these can transport us back to trauma time, our bodies feeling just like we are at the original scene of the crime or trauma. Van der Volk and colleagues explain (17):

> 'Trauma doesn't just act as a releasing agent for symptoms. Rather, the memory of the trauma acts like a foreign body, which, long after its entry, continues to be an agent at work. Like a splinter that causes an infection, the body's response to the foreign object becomes the problem, more than the object itself.'

Research about stress and trauma has now shown that trauma is stored in our bodies and that our autonomic nervous system is responsible for the symptoms experienced due to the body's sympathetic dominance (fight, flight and freeze). This can be thought of as the body's heating system; its engine is in the form of action, ready to respond to the threat.

Any approach that will help must bring online the body's ability to 'cool' and allow the 'engine' to enter the resting state. This highlights the power of the parasympathetic nervous system or our 'relaxation response'. This is undertaken within therapeutic care relationships.

For children, we need to be able to help them understand these normal physiological changes which happen in our bodies; in a blink of an eye, our bodies decide how to respond. When the child is in a place of safety, we can help them understand (child-friendly psycho-education) to increase their awareness of what happens.

The use of metaphor is beneficial for everyone to develop a way of relating to different physiological states, a 'fire-breathing dragon' whose flames need to be cooled. This means calming their physiological reactions – soothing their fight-flight-freeze response, so they can return to their natural state of being a 'colourful unicorn'.

Often, there is a notion that these can be 'taught' educationally; but these need to be experienced and modelled within a relationship. Just as a nurturing parent would calm their child's nervous system, we need to be able to do this for the children. This could be thought of as providing an alternative attachment relationship which, over time, supports the child through being able to ensure the child feels safe, soothed, seen, and secure. Adults model the capacity to self-regulate (so they can co-regulate).

To do this, we cannot become the 'Hulk', 'fire-breathing dragon', or be dysregulated. We want the children to experience our ability to regulate ourselves repeatedly. This means we validate feelings but model emotional management and good affect regulation. We demonstrate how we deal with feelings of anger, for example, and show in the moment, minute-by-minute interactions, how we do this, for example, 'I am going to take a deep breath; I can feel things are getting difficult'. It is all about providing this through the felt experiences in the relationship.

Safety first

In 1889 Pierre Janet was the first to suggest a triple-phased model of recovery (17) from trauma impacts, resurrected by Judith Herman. She wrote (18):

> 'Safety is essential to the process of healing.'

This model was thus, first, safety and stabilisation; second, working through trauma; and, third, reconnecting to meaningful activities in life.

The journey for a child or adult (we may need to acknowledge our own developmental experiences as a carer) is not linear, going seamlessly from safety and stabilisation, not having to return to safety at times.

What does 'safety and stabilisation' mean in practice? We have been thinking about this since the start of this chapter. This is about creating an experience for the child, which is the opposite of being trauma-organised and being trauma- and attachment-responsive. There is predictability and consistency, which slowly but surely becomes internalised by the child, alongside a focus on developing coping through our relational practice.

Sometimes, there is a belief that we must avoid therapeutically implementing and maintaining boundaries, but this is often the biggest error; we cannot be a bystander when working with the traumatised child. To be experienced as the giving, permissive adult does not and will not internalise safe, empathic caring. On the other hand, a boundary-limiting adult in a therapeutic relationship provides containment, anxiety management and the context to work through relational difficulties.

It is also not about staying in a position of neutrality or passivity. As carers, we need to develop a capacity to harness our sense of empowerment within this approach, be reflective and mindful at the moment, understand what needs to be responded to, and not become unable to think and act appropriately.

The importance of the relationship

This chapter has not been about a psychologist or psychotherapist providing an intervention; this has been all about 24/7 relational care provided to children who are cared for. Often, it is not about helping the child get back to something; it is often about creating something new that takes patience, care and understanding. This responsive attuned care over time can allow, as one child described, 'I have been on guard all my life; I think this is not needed anymore'.

When we come into the world, we need adults to see us, notice, and respond in particular ways, which is not about what we say but how we are in the moment – our gaze, our felt safeness when the infant is in distress, our ability to soothe and calm.

We have been highlighting the importance of both biology and psychology. Focusing on and understanding neurobiology seems complex. However, this opens a new paradigm for understanding the natural and normal biologically driven responses, often outside the child's conscious awareness. Similarly, for the practitioner, this provides an insight into what we may consciously or unconsciously bring into the relationship.

Similarly, as the carer, we need to be aware of our triggers, past painful experiences and subsequently activated bodily states. If we are not prepared, these can make us more likely to leave our self-regulated state. We are responsible for identifying and effectively responding to these changes.

Often, neurobiology, attachment and trauma are seen as separate fields. I have been seeking to illuminate the critical importance of encapsulating the understanding from these areas to develop practice and approaches that can assist those children and young people.

As I have explained, attachment and early developmental experiences are often the templates for how we relate to others; our autonomic nervous system plays an essential role in the symptoms and lasting responses to what we have experienced. Our mind and body do not realise it is no longer in a situation of fear without resolution.

This operates out of sight and unconsciously (neuroception) and can bring to the care relationship lots of highs and lows, often termed as being on the 'therapeutic rollercoaster' (19). One of the first principles is accepting that being alongside and bearing witness to a child's pain and trauma creates powerful feelings in us. As Pawl counselled (20):

> 'It is not possible to work on behalf of human beings
> to try to help them without having powerful feelings
> aroused in yourself.'

Providing care can be painful at times, 'what gives light must endure burning' (21), but this does not need to become harmful or contagion to us in the role of carer. Take this illustration:

> *Example 3*
>
> I had left the home five hours ago after being on shift overnight. I keep thinking about what happened, it feels like something has 'hitched' a lift inside of me. It's confusing, I want to enjoy my day off, but I feel I cannot escape the fear that was around last night, I know it wasn't mine. The child looked so scared even although they were safe. Why do I feel unsafe when I know I am safe?

Just as we want the children to develop and maximise their ability to increasingly utilise both self-regulation (affect regulation) and inter-regulation (to be able to gain support from others), we need to model this capacity for ourselves and be aware of how it feels to have access to these two crucial ways of maintaining and keeping us within our window of tolerance.

Sometimes, it can feel like the child is using us as a screen to project all their anger, sadness, and foreboding (projective identification), how we identify and make sense of what was being given and the need to be clear about what we are transferring back (counter-transference).

We bring ourselves into every moment with a child; this can be all that is conscious to us, that we know about ourselves and the foundations of our responses. There is also so much that can be considered outside our awareness, which we can strive to understand. Therefore, we need to emphasise that just as the child requires an environment around them that can be understanding, open and emotionally containing, so do we; spaces where supervision can create a secure base where we can bravely identify and notice our blind spots and responses.

From the onset, this seeks to place importance on developing a framework of understanding that assists us as practitioners and in parallel with the children in our care which builds upon earlier work (22).

The mindful carer

Most of this text has focused on how we as adults are the therapeutic agents of change. To be 'therapeutic', there needs to be an ability to harness these primary ingredients for successful recovery for children.

This is not only about having knowledge about the impacts of trauma but how to use this understanding to create experiences which gradually support the child's recovery. Some of these qualities are:

- *Humanness*: our ability to connect to the child, to be empathically attuned. We need to assess our state and feeling of connectedness openly and transparently.

- *Empathy*: we can 'walk in the shoes of the child' and be able to connect to the child's state of being accurate.

- *Being mindful*: we are engaged, committed, and caring.

- *Our stuff*: we are aware of the importance of being aware of what we are bringing into the interactions with the child and the potential of these to be healing interactions.

- *Boundaries and structure*: we are comfortable with boundary maintenance to ensure consistency and predictability.

- *Attachment*: we know that this might be both longed for and dreaded. Some children can experience relationship closeness as a trigger for danger.

- *Collaboration, empowerment and problem solving*: we need to stay grounded and in a 'thinking state' to ensure we can work with the child who often has experienced limited choices, to ensure they understand they have choices.

All the above requires us to cultivate reflective thinking and be in the present moment, be available physically and have emotional responsiveness.

Relational breaches and repair

I often start my work with children by communicating that there will be 'disappointments' when I might miss something important. Things will not be perfect, but I will always ensure I am 'good enough'.

This communication is on multiple levels, emphasising that, as with all relationships, there will be times of tension, miscommunication, missteps, and errors. However, if we can acknowledge these, not only will we get through these situations, but these can be 'therapeutic' as they often provide for the child the experiences of 'successful' repair. As a principle, this is so important.

For this reason, care systems, not only at the direct level of the school, fostering family or residential staff team, are part of a larger culture which need to have proactive approaches in place to respond to relational ruptures transparently, openly, and safely. This might require supportive supervision and support, which requires a culture which encourages openness and transparency.

Conclusion

The power of the relationship cannot be understated. This is not about using a specific strategy or technique but about using our very way of being within the moment-to-moment interactions with children. Children and young people frequently describe the powerful, helpful experiences from the calm, regulated adult, who can soothe and regulate them during a period of crisis for a child.

This ability to receive the child's communications which is everything transmitted to us from the child, the majority of which is non-verbal and through behaviour and proactively respond, is a crucial ability that must be kept online within ourselves.

This approach is based on understanding the elements often needed to understand complex trauma fully. The three strands of attachment, trauma and dissociation are all connected to how we respond to 'fear'. This can provide a framework for understanding the normal biological responses of children who have experienced complex trauma and a clear understanding of the need to work with the biological responses developed for survival.

We need to act as a container for what is brought to us by the child by providing a secure, sensitive, and responsive attunement, regardless of the affective storms that we may experience.

Attaining this depends on our developing abilities to maintain being mindful and self-regulated adults. This, in turn, assists us in being able to be present in a relationally sensitive manner, which can create the environment within which recovery from complex trauma can occur.

* *The three indented examples in this chapter (on pages 42, 43 and 46) are fictional descriptions of the experiences of the author in his support for therapeutic teams.*

References

(1) Cozolino, Louis J., *The Neuroscience of Human Relationships: Attachment and the Developing Social Brain*. New York: W.W. Norton & Company, 2014.

(2) Bloom, S. L., 'The Sanctuary Model: Developing generic inpatient Programs for the treatment of psychological trauma'. In M.B. Williams and J.F. Sommer (Eds) *Handbook of Post-Traumatic Therapy, A Practical Guide to Intervention, Treatment, and Research*. Greenwood Publishing, 2014.

(3) Cloitre, M., 'ICD–11 complex post–traumatic stress disorder: simplifying diagnosis in trauma populations'. *The British Journal of Psychiatry*, 216 (3) 129–131, 2020. doi:10.1192/bjp.2020.43

(4) Bowlby, J., *Attachment and Loss: Volume 3. Loss*. New York, NY: Basic Books, 1980.

(5) Bowlby, J., *Attachment and Loss: Volume 1. Attachment*. New York, NY: Basic Books, 1969.

(6) Bowlby, J., *Attachment and Loss: Volume 2. Separation*. New York, NY: Basic Books, 1973.

(7) Bowlby, J., *A Secure Base: Parent–child attachment and healthy human development*. New York, NY: Basic Books, 1988.

(8) Ainsworth, M. D. S., Blehar, M. C., Waters, E. and Wall, S., *Patterns of Attachment: Psychological Study of the Strange Situation*. Hillsdale, NJ: Erlbaum, 1978.

(9) Main, M. and Solomon, J., 'Discovery of a new, insecure-disorganized/disoriented attachment pattern'. In T. B. Brazelton and M. Yogman (Eds) *Affective Development in Infancy*. New Jersey: Norwood, pp. 95–124, 1986.

(10) Main, M. and Hesse, E., 'Parents' unresolved traumatic experiences are related to infant disorganized attachment status: Is frightened and/or frightening parental behavior the linking mechanism?' In M. T. Greenberg, D. Cicchetti and E. M. Cummings (Eds) *Attachment in the Preschool Years: Theory, research, and intervention*. Chicago: The University of Chicago Press, pp. 161–182, 1990.

(11) Heijer, D. A., *Nothing You Don't Already Know: Remarkable reminders about meaning, purpose, and self-realization* (1st Ed). CreateSpace Independent Publishing Platform, 2018.

(12) Bowlby, J., 'Forty-four juvenile thieves: their characters and home life', *The International Journal of Psychoanalysis*, 1944/1946.

(13) Felitti, V. J., 'Adverse childhood experiences and adult health', *Academic paediatrics* 9 (3) 131–132, 2009.

(14) Turney, K. and Wildeman, C., 'Adverse childhood experiences among children placed in and adopted from foster care: Evidence from a nationally representative survey', *Child Abuse & Neglect*, 64, 117–129, 2017.

(15) Siegel, D. J., *The Developing Mind: Toward a neurobiology of interpersonal experience.* New York: Guilford Press, 1999.

(16) Freud, S. and Bruer, J., *Physical Mechanism of Hysterical Phenomenon*, 1896.

(17) van der Kolk, B.A., Brown, P. and van der Hart, O., 'Pierre Janet on post-traumatic stress'. *J Trauma Stress*, 2, 365–378, 1989.

(18) Herman, J., *Trauma and Recovery*. New York: Basic Books, 2015.

(19) Chu, J. A., *Rebuilding Shattered Lives: Treating complex PTSD and dissociative disorders*. John Wiley & Sons, 2011.

(20) Pawl, J., 'On supervision'. In R. Shahmoon-Shanok, L. Gilkerson and E. Fenichel (Eds) *Reflective Supervision: A relationship for learning*. Arlington, VA: Washington, pp. 41–49, 1995.

(21) Frankl, V. E., *Man's Search for Meaning*, Boston: Beacon Press, 2006.

(22) Cross, R., 'Interpersonal childhood trauma and the use of the therapeutic community in recovery'. *Therapeutic Communities: The International Journal of Therapeutic Communities*, 33 (1) 3953, 2012. doi:10.1108/09641861211286311

Our vision
Every child and
can grow, flouris
their potential.
ur mission
Working with our
partner agencies,
and young people,
ange of
informed, high impa
leading evidence-ba
which deliver transfo
outcomes – turning
lives around.
I wish for children in care to fulfil all their hopes & dreams
Five Rivers.

Healing Systems

Five Rivers created a project in collaboration with social workers and commissioners to have the child in mind and asked what they wanted for children in care. Hope was one of the popular answers.

CHAPTER 4

The Needs of Children and Adolescents Through Adulthood: A Developmental Approach

Camea Peca

Introduction

I have worked for more than years of with children all ages, from many different backgrounds and in many different countries; if someone were to ask me what is the most important thing that children need it would be one word – love. However, love is not the only thing that is needed; it would be best to expand the answer to include 'secure attachment' which is built on the foundation of love. We are born into a relationship, and the safety, stability and love that is modelled in this primary relationship not only supports the child in healthy developmental growth but also lays the foundation for all future relationships. Parents, caregivers and adults are the primary providers of the blueprint that will be encoded for the child that will carry them through to adulthood. In addition, co-regulation* and the ability to regulate will provide a crucial role in the child's development. This chapter will explain the importance of safety, stability, love through attachment, modeling, and regulation as the key ingredients for healthy development.

What's love got to do with it?

The foundation of all healthy development is attachment which is fueled by love of the mother or caregiver for the infant. Although we know that this love is far from perfect, especially when the needs of the infant and then the child are vast and unrelenting, it is necessary for growth and development. Neurochemically, the oxytocin that is produced in the primary relationship is what feeds the nervous system of both the parent and the child. The first relationship should ideally provide a sense of security and safety facilitated by the caregiver as she or he responds to the infant's distress signals.

The two of them regulate the affect of the other by transactional patterns of regulation. This is referred to as attunement and operates like a dialogue or dance, mostly comprised of non-verbal facial expressions and noises. This process is supported neurobiologically with mirror neurons with which the infant is born. The mirror neurons combine inner and outer experiences, resulting in copying and connective gestures. They relay the message, 'I see you and you see me'. By 18 months, the child will understand the goal of action without seeing it. These messages and signals are the crossroads of sensory motor, somatic and executive function. They are also the foundation of cognitive and emotional understanding that leads to empathy.

When the infant and then child is attuned and attended to from birth they are more likely to start to build a secure attachment which is crucial to development. Research seems to indicate that our attachment style is developed early (by three years of age), although it can be changed later in life. This attachment style is the basis of our adult relationships, specifically as it relates to comfort with affection, intimacy. Individuals who are securely attached as children tend to be securely attached in their adult relationships as well. They feel secure in their partner's love and they feel that they can trust them, gaining comfort and security. Individuals who are insecurely attached at this point tend to be insecure and anxious about their relationships when they are adults, and may try to avoid being too attached to any one person. The impact of attachment style is long lasting, affecting the relationships that we have with our own children. It is important for adults to be aware of their early experiences of attachment, as well as parenting, specifically for this reason.

While it is not the intention to delve into attachment styles and the nuances between them in great detail, it is worth noting that the attachment style of the child has an impact on the way the child behaves in the classroom when they reach school age, as well as social and emotional development. In the classroom, the securely attached child is commonly seen to be engaged with content, concentrating on tasks, and is appropriately engaged with the teacher and other students.

- The avoidantly attached child** can be withdrawn, quiet, and anxious. This child may often go under the radar, sitting at the back, never asking a question, and never 'a problem' – essentially, invisible.

- The anxiously attached child*** is often not focused and insecure, both with his or her academic ability and in his or her relationships with teachers and peers. This is a child who always has his or her hand up, asking questions, and also needs that affirmation relationally, that is, soothing or affirmation from the relationship or caregiver.

- The disorganised attached child is often described as a trouble maker and appears both angry and depressed. This child has difficulty following directions and has a very short fuse, as well as difficulty with peer relationships.

With all of this said, in order for the child to be on a neurotypical development trajectory the parenting and the attachment relationship does not need to be perfect. Winnicott (1) suggested that you only have to be 'good *enough*' as a parent, which equates to roughly 50 percent or more of the time. Parents actually help build the child's resilience by not constantly responding to their cues, as long as the child has had enough experiences of knowing that the adult going to be there eventually. The same is true of misreading their cues. It is important that there is communication or a dialogue and the child learns over time that the caregiver is going to be there, maybe not all the time, but when they need it.

As children grow older the developmental need shifts from having their basic physiological needs met to attuning more to their emotional needs – that adults are working to fill and refill children's 'emotional cup'. This includes helping children to organise their emotions and letting them know the delight they have in welcoming them back, protecting, comforting, and understanding them. The key for caregivers is to remain strong and calm. It is about knowing when to encourage the child to go out into the world and how to be available to welcome them back. It is crucial that caregivers learn to identify the child's needs, because misreading them or, worse, missing them altogether can cause pain and frustration. We all know how uncomfortable it can be to be held too close, when we want to be out exploring or kept at a distance. Likewise, there are times when we need emotional support or simply to be with someone who is bigger, stronger, wiser and kind, who we can trust to understand when we're feeling lost, confused or out of control. It is vital to understand that a child's cues look different with age. When a child misbehaves, the cause is often rooted in how safe and secure he or she is feeling and is an indicator that he or she is moving into a dysregulated state – that is, the child has a poor ability to manage emotional responses or to keep them within an acceptable range of typical emotional reactions.

When children are stuck in a state of dysregulation they need adults to support them in moving out of this state and to offer them co-regulation. Mirror neurons will support the child in internalising the offers of co-regulation from the caregivers when they are dysregulated. Co-regulation starts with the adult being regulated first, but once this is achieved, some simple suggestions include listening, being aware of tone, using eye contact, moving closer, offering affection if appropriate (this can including, rocking, holding, stroking, patting), using simple sentences or words and using a model to bring a child back to 'ground'. One such model is known as the PACE model.

The PACE model

Baylin and Hughes (2) suggest parents and caregivers use the PACE model to encourage healthy development and secure attachments. PACE stands for:

- **P**layfulness, which also includes enjoyment, being silly and having fun with the child

- **A**cceptance, which speaks to the aforementioned interpretation of behaviour as a form of communication, and reserving judgement. This is in line with the thinking that by the time a child reaches a point where they are acting out behaviourally they have already moved into a state of dysregulation and are adapting or mitigating to get back into a balanced place the best way they know how

- **C**uriosity – this includes being interested in the emotions behind the behaviour as well as allowing space for the child to explore these feelings

- **E**mpathy, which includes letting the child know you are with them and understand what they are experiencing. Remember that the adult cannot access their own ability to be empathetic if he or she is not in a regulated state. The adult being regulated is just as important as regulating for the child; the child cannot out-regulate the adult. We regulate each other's internal biochemistry, emotions and behaviour by conscious and unconscious mechanisms, socially.

The importance of the adult as a model

The neural systems organise our attachment, emotional, and social communication. The brain is a social organ of adaptation and it is built through interaction with others. When referring to the blueprint we are really referring to the internal working models that the infant and then child, wire in unconsciously. They are the prototypes that children will use to frame their internal and external world view. Porges (3) describes this process as 'neuroception' and it is characterised as being an unconscious process. We impact each other's internal biological state and influence in the long-term construction of each other's brains, through the transferring of states which become templates. Although this is crucial in the first five years, modeling does not lose its importance as children grow into teens.

In the first three years of life the infant and then child is constantly looking to the environment and, most important, the adults to develop models for relational patterns, emotional patterns, cognitive patterns, and physical patterns. All of these patterns are developed through unconscious observation of the environment and the people in the environment. If the adults are safe and provide regulated, although not perfect modeling, the templates that will be formed will be that 'I am loved and people are loving'. Templates also include the way in which the world is viewed which in this case would be, 'The world is, overall, a safe place and the adults in my life meet my needs'. However, if there is a history of early childhood adversity and trauma the templates that are formed are very different. This can cause developmental challenges both when it is time for the child to separate and distinguish itself in toddlerhood and then again in adolescence. This corresponds with two major episodes of brain growth, age zero to four and adolescence.

The expansion of the cortex in primates corresponds with increasing larger groups. This allows for safety in numbers, task specialization such as hunting, gathering and caretaking. Children enter more complicated social groups both at the start of school and later in adolescent peer groups. Both of these time periods are marked with the child venturing out more into the social world but needing the safe base of the parents to come back to as well. In both periods we also see the parallel of language and brain growth allowing for the development of higher levels of symbolic and abstract functioning.

By the time the children reach adolescence they are looking for confirmation of these templates and so will be attracted to other adolescents and teens that hold the same templates. This can lead to frustration for the parents as they see their teens entering relationships that are similar to those that they have engaged in or left.

Adolescence and the teenage years

Psycho-education (that is, learning and understanding about mental health and well-being) around templating and understanding how early templating and attachment impact relational choices for teens is important. It is also important for parents and caregivers to understand the developmental stages that adolescents traverse and the need to move through the second period of separation and distinguishing themselves from others. Many parents experience this as a rejection and withdraw love and attention during this time. The crucial piece that is often missing is the understanding that as in toddlerhood, the child still needs to return to the safe base. They also need the safety and stability in the relationship more than ever as well as the regulated adult. Developmentally, this stage is shrouded with dysregulation and there is a default to mitigation strategies, to try and get back into balance through substances, self-harm, and sexual relationships. During this time the modeling of healthy ways to regain balance and regulation is crucial. The caregivers need to be present to recognise the dysregulation, identify emotions, and offer healthy strategies to regulate.

The development of the frontal lobe and executive function skills is also rapid during both of these periods. (The executive function is the mental processes that enable us to plan, focus attention, remember instructions, and juggle multiple tasks successfully.) In the early period of development, children need the modeling of the skills which include emotional control, managing and expressing feelings, being creative and flexible in thinking, planning, working through frustration, and impulse control. The adults in the child's life need to be able to model these skills with their own behaviour and to step back to allow the child to work through the challenges, not coming to the rescue to save or abandon him or her. Both the rescuer and the abandoner will do the child a disservice and the latter will not have the experience of relationships to support them. The same parenting skills are needed for teenagers as they move into new social groups and situations.

More often than not, parents have an expectation that teens are able to function as adults when it comes to executive function but the frontal lobes are not fully developed until mid-20s. Much of the mis-attunement during this period is due to the caregivers' lack of awareness of where the teenage brain has actually reached developmentally. It is also worth noting that if there has been any developmental trauma, the part of the brain that was supposed to grow during that period may not have developed, leaving the child neuro-developmentally behind. Often, there are high expectations, when it comes to self-regulation and impulse control from the children that have experienced the most trauma during these periods. If the younger tasks were never achieved, they will not have the foundation to build on and the caregivers will need to go back and model and build these first.

The causes of developmental delay

So what prevents a child from being able to fulfil their appropriate physical and emotional milestones and the impact on the deficit?

Early life adverse experiences and environments are the biggest indicators and cause of delay in developmental processes, including meeting physical and emotional milestones. The environment has a profound impact on emotional and physical growth, particularly during the first five years. The environments that have an impact on development are not just the environments where there has been abuse or a major traumatic event. Although childhood trauma can have a major impact on the ability of children to grow and thrive into adulthood, it is often not the actual events that are the cause of the long-term delay. It is more commonly the experience of living in an environment where the adults are chronically dysregulated. This can be due to trauma or their experience of living in stressful situations where they are never able to get back into their own regulated state. Often, co-regulation has not been modelled or offered so the child has to self-soothe or is left abandoned in the dysregulated state. If left in this state for extended periods of time, we see a profound impact on several developmental processes and, in extreme cases, neuro-developmental freeze. When the child is chronically dysregulated the parts of the brain that are most impacted developmentally are the pre-frontal cortex and frontal lobes that are vital for learning, as well as emotional development. Children who are unable to move out of dysregulation successfully often suffer in terms of their peer relationships as they lack empathy and impulse control. Our brains not only communicate to both hemispheres what is happening at the top (the brain) down to the rest of the nervous system and body, but we also have horizontal hemispheres communicating with each other through the corpus callosum and need both sides of the brain to connect, to learn and develop socially.

Dysregulated children can also struggle with more common developmental delays, such as failing to reach milestones with maths and reading. This makes perfect sense as they would not have been regulated enough to grow and access the parts of the brain that perform these more complicated tasks. Much like the caregivers in the child's life, the teachers also need to provide a regulated environment and understand that when the child is dysregulated they cannot learn effectively. Both in the classroom and the home the primary goal should always be regulation.

Some of the environments that produce dysregulation, do so through small repeated cumulative events. These include but are not limited to chaotic environments, aggressive environments, and punitive environments. These environments are characterized by inconsistent practices and instability which means that the nervous system of the child is not able to move from hyper-vigilance into the relaxed state that is needed for growth and development. The aggressive environment is characterised by rules coming before relationships. In punitive environments there is a demand for performance that is valued more highly than attachment or relationship. The rules for operating are constantly in flux, based on the annoyance of those in charge. All of these environments are also lacking in the child trusting adults to be safe and provide for the child's emotional and co-regulatory needs.

The impact of parental regulation and dysregulation

The reciprocal interactions of passing dysregulation from the child to the parent can be damaging for both the child and the parent. The parent, physiologically dysregulated because of the child's difficult behaviour, may benefit from developing physiologically regulating responses to avoid higher levels of parenting stress that could also be related to lower parental attachment (4). Attachment theory supports attachment being built through reciprocal interactions between the parent and the child (5). Historically, these reciprocal interactions have been studied in terms of the passing back and forth of emotional states but not physiological states. However, the more able the parent is able to track their own emotional state which is more commonly known as interoceptive awareness, the greater their ability to navigate normal parenting challenges as well as more challenging behaviours.

van der Kolk (6) has called for the development of the ability to to identify, access, understand, and respond appropriately to the patterns of internal signals (interoceptive awareness), especially when working with populations who have experienced trauma. Fay (7) has suggested starting with the body for the healing of trauma and insecure attachments. Baylin and Hughes's (2) dyadic developmental psychotherapy describes self-regulation as one of the key functions damaged in trauma. (This psychotherapy is attachment-based and designed for children and their caregivers where there has been significant emotional and attachment trauma/neglect.)

The damage is a result of lack of an interoceptive model from the parents early in life, resulting in stunted neurobiology. It can be surmised that interoceptive awareness may be the foundation of the other regulatory systems that need to come on board in terms of relational healing for the child. Moilanen et al (8) suggested parent socialization and the ability of the parent to regulate effectively are key in terms of the child's development of his or her own regulatory functions. This includes, but is not limited to, the child developing interoceptive awareness then neurological arousal. Kanbara and Fukunaga (9) identified the importance of interoceptive awareness in emotional processing and the relational impact on noticing the emotional states of others. One of the ways that the parents support the development of the child is through their own interoceptive modeling and the overall atmosphere created in the home, whether it is the biological home or the foster home. The parent–child role–modeling of interoceptive awareness is also core to the validation of the child's sensory-emotional experience that builds both emotional health and attachment capacity in the child.

Williams and Woodruff-Borden (10) examined the effect parental self-regulation has on children's anxiety levels and found that the parents' ability to regulate had a significant impact on children's level of anxiety. The strongest impact of the effect was unsupportive parenting and the detrimental effects of this parenting. This also confirms the parental role in modeling and their response when faced with the maladaptive behaviours characteristic of children who have experienced trauma. The National Traumatic Stress Network (11) identified four evidence-based interventions, all of which address internal awareness, regulation of internal processes, and the use of relationship and attachment to promote growth and healing.

Summary

The key to healthy development starts with the parent or caregiver. This includes building their own regulatory capacity. When the adults are regulated, children and later teens will feel safe in their ability to express their needs and emotions without fear. Simple communication normalising feelings and frustrations without judgement and attack are vital to building communication skills later on in the teen years. Remember that these lessons and such communication can only be absorbed in the regulated state, so reflection can only occur after regulation. When children are dysregulated they only need the presence of the co-regulator to get their bodies back in a balanced state. Knowing their adults show up for them creates safety and trust. This safety in the relationship will lead to the ability to not only question and explore challenges but to ask for support in navigating through them. This process starts with modeling regulation and understanding developmental stages and the needs of the child in each stage.

Notes

*Co-regulation is the process in which the parent or caregiver assists in regulating the state of the of child by attuning to their needs while remaining regulated themselves. Another way to think about this is a captain that remains calm during the storm whilst the other crewmates are scared or nervous from the storm. By remaining calm they are able to come back into a state where they can do what they need to do for the ship to navigate the storm.

** Avoidantly attached children have not had the opportunity to be attended to when they experience distress and may have been neglected or responded to harshly. As a result of these early experiences they may appear to be more self-sufficient, will often shut down emotions or disconnect from them, and will in turn reject support from adults as the adults have not shown up for them in the past.

*** Anxiously attached children may not have had consistent parenting responses early in life, sometimes they would have been met with love and affection and other times with coldness/rejection. As a result of these early experiences, they may appear to be clingy or fearful when the caregiver leaves and may be hard to console when they get upset.

References

(1) Winnicott, D., *The Maturational Process and the Facilitating Environment*. New York: Int. Univ. Press, 1965.

(2) Baylin, J. and Hughes, D., *The Neurobiology of Attachment-Focused Therapy: Enhancing Connection and Trust in the Treatment of Children and Adolescents*. New York: W.W. Norton & Company, 2016.

(3) Porges, S.W., *The Polyvagal Theory: Neurophysiological Foundations of Emotions, Attachment, Communication and Self-regulation*. New York, NY: W.W. Norton & Company, 2011.

(4) Kain, K. and Terrell, S., *Nurturing Resilience: Helping Clients Move Forward from Developmental Trauma: An Integrative Somatic Approach*. Berkley, CA: North Atlantic Books, 2018.

(5) Bowlby, J., *A Secure Base: Parent–Child Attachment and Healthy Human Development*. New York: Basic Books, 1998.

(6) van der Kolk, B. A., *The Body Keeps the Score: Brain, Mind, and Body in the Healing of Trauma*. New York: Viking, 2014.

(7) Fay, D., *Attachment–based Yoga and Meditation for Trauma Recovery: Simple, Safe and Effective Practices for Therapy*. New York, NY: W.W. Norton and Company, 2017.

(8) Moilanen, K. L., Rasmussen, K. E. and Padilla-Walker, L. M., 'Bidirectional associations between self–regulation and parenting styles in early adolescence', *Journal of Research on Adolescence*, 2, p. 246, 2015.

(9) Kanbara, K. and Fukunaga, M., 'Links among emotional awareness, somatic awareness and autonomic homeostatic processing', *Biopsychosocial Medicine*, 10, 2016.

(10) Williams, S. and Woodruff-Borden, J., 'Parent emotion socialization practices and child self-regulation as predictors of child anxiety: The mediating role of cardiac variability', *Child Psychiatry and Human Development*, 46, pp. 512–22, 2015.

(11) Child Welfare Committee, National Child Traumatic Stress Network, Child Welfare Trauma, *Training Toolkit: Comprehensive Guide* (3rd edition). Los Angeles, CA & Durham, NC: National Center for Child Traumatic Stress, 2013.

Children shaping change and their voices being heard

Five Rivers Child Care helped children in care meet with senior government officials, including the Children's Commissioner, to express their experiences in care and to raise awareness of their aspirations. Their art projection in collaboration with Plymouth University was projected on to civic buildings in various settings.

CHAPTER 5

What Looked-After Children Need to Succeed Educationally

Perdita Mousley

Introduction

In the 1980s, two studies revealed an alarming situation: that many children leaving care had poor educational attainments (1, 2). At this time, the education of looked-after children in the United Kingdom was given low priority in care plans. The poor outcomes of individuals, who spent time in care as children, have been confidently linked to educational failure (3). Over the last 20 years research determined that outcomes for children are influenced by the interplay of associated factors with education deemed as important as living situations on children's welfare (4).

The Children Act 1989 introduced a duty to prepare looked-after children for adult life. The Act was followed by the Children Act 2004, which was the first legislative document to emphasise the need for local authorities to promote the educational achievement of looked-after children. The importance of education and the value of listening to children in care are highlighted in the legislation. Schooling is vital in enabling looked-after children to make the best of adverse circumstances by offering opportunities for educational success and in presenting them with alternative supporting relationships, with peers and teaching staff. In preparing looked-after children for adult life, schools are required to support children to develop the skills they need for learning, life and work, with a strong emphasis on the development of well-rounded individuals who are confident, responsible, and valuable contributors to society.

Preparing looked-after children for adulthood is especially difficult because many of them find it difficult to focus and persist in the present, let alone think about their future. However, by emphasising that education is the biggest social driver in society and the best form of protection for looked-after children, educators can provide them with positive influences. Enjoyment in school is directly linked to a child's ability to learn and achieve but children's well-being also provides a solid foundation for their future well-being as adults. Children in care do not have different aspirations to other children, as they, too, want a good home, job and to be financially secure. By achieving at school, they can enjoy these aspects of adult life.

The majority of research into the educational achievement of looked-after children focuses on explaining their low achievement in education or their educational failure instead of their educational success (5). Rather than continuing to identify and analyse educational underachievement this chapter focuses on the educational opportunities that encourage looked-after children to succeed. Although looked-after children share many commonalities with other children, because of their experiences and circumstances they generally have additional and specific support needs within the education system.

Understanding the nature of looked-after children and the impact of entering the care system is imperative for appropriate support to be provided to these children. Before describing support mechanisms and factors that encourage looked-after children to progress and achieve at school, the next section considers the impact of adversities on their educational experiences.

Educational experiences

In 2021 in the United Kingdom there were approximately 102,000 looked-after children, an increase of 10,000 children over a five-year period, since 2016. Across the United Kingdom the most common placement for a looked-after child is living in foster care. Currently, three quarters of looked-after children are placed with foster carers and cared for in a family-based setting. The majority of these children are educated in mainstream schools, a term that covers a wide variety of schools, including maintained schools, academies, free schools, grammar schools and faith schools. Mainstream schools report a lack of understanding in supporting and planning the education of looked-after children. There are concerns that, due to this lack of understanding, schools are missing an opportunity to help improve the future prospects of these children. At worst, a picture of damaging educational experiences results for looked-after children, including academic failure and exclusion.

In certain circumstances, for example, a child choosing not to live with foster carers, a child who experiences a series of failed foster placements or when specialist skills are required for dealing with concerning behaviours, alternative placements such as residential schools, children's homes, semi-independent living, secure units, and other residential settings are the preferred placement option.

Many children spend less than a year looked after, consequently, during a school year many children change where and with whom they live. Placement changes including frequent care moves, resulting in changes of school, are known to result in a loss of curricula and supportive networks, which hinders children's educational progress and can lead to school absences. Looked-after children require stability and security, a need that is significantly diminished with changes of residential placements and schools. The initial move from the family home into a care placement can be a traumatic experience for many children as placement changes can be sudden and often unanticipated. Moving home for anyone is regarded as being decidedly stressful but for children, moving home can become a regular occurrence that understandably is accompanied by extreme emotional distress due to the possible breakdown of the previous placement and the uncertainty of their new living arrangements. Children who move regularly miss out on teaching and learning which puts them at a disadvantage in terms of educational progress and reinforces their unwillingness, possibly even fear, of attending school. Within this vicious cycle lies the punishment of exclusion, which only compounds issues for children who lack the desire to attend school in the first place.

Educational outcomes

The poor outcomes for looked-after children are well documented. In 2019, 37 per cent of looked-after children attained the nationally expected standard, or above, in reading, writing and mathematics at the end of key stage 2 (11 years of age) compared to 65 per cent of non-looked-after children (6). By the end of key stage 4 (16 years of age) the picture is much worse as the average Attainment 8 score for looked-after children is 19.1 compared to 44.6 for non-looked-after children. Attainment 8 measures the average achievement of pupils in up to eight qualifications, including English (double weighted if language and literature are taken), maths (double weighted), three additional qualifications, including the English Baccalaureate (Ebacc), and three qualifications, either GCSEs or non-GCSEs, that are included on the Department for Education approved list. With regard to education and/or employment destinations 19 per cent of care leavers participate in further education and just six per cent go on to higher education compared with 38 per cent of all young people who progress to further or higher education (7).

The figures above describe how looked-after children fare less well in school than non-looked-after children. Looking behind the statistics, several researchers provide a concentrated awareness of the difficulties experienced by looked-after children from the perspective of children themselves (8, 9). Children describe many factors as contributing to their difficulties to learn in school, these factors include pre-care social, economic and structural adversities, such as poor housing, unemployment, poverty, parents with mental health issues, and domestic violence. These disadvantages are compounded by experiences of abuse, neglect, violence and/or trauma. Sixty per cent of looked-after children enter the care system as a result of maltreatment (10). Maltreatment is associated with a range of negative outcomes that can adversely change educational attainment. Children who have been exposed to maltreatment and adverse experiences can display a profile of significant maladjustment impacting on developmental progress, learning ability and behaviour as well as memory deficits, difficulties with communication, abstract thinking and social problems.

What limits achievement

As a result of painful and confusing experiences looked-after children demonstrate poor pro-social skills, as well as aggressive, disruptive or withdrawn behaviour. Attachment issues are also associated with low educational attainment and are particularly identifiable in looked-after children. Children with insecure or disorganised attachments have been found to show a number of challenges that directly or indirectly have an impact on learning and attainment, including internalising problems, demonstrating less resilience when faced with challenges, lower language competency, poor social self-control, and problems with peer relationships in childhood.

It is well established that many looked-after children have experienced difficulties in their birth families, schools and neighbourhoods. This exposure to weak or broken attachments can lead to long-term difficulties in developing secure attachments. Secure attachments are thought to be responsible for the human stress response, which facilitates the development of a child's coping strategies. When considering attachment in relation to education and learning, a connection has been identified between early attachment patterns and responses to learning. A child with disorganised attachment exhibits a different learning profile to a securely attached child. Children with attachment disorders demonstrate intense anxiety, limited use of imagination, difficulty in trusting authority figures (school leaders and teaching staff), difficulties accepting 'not knowing', and underachievement. Children may also exhibit resistance, avoidance, distraction or aggression, which may be the result of them being overwhelmed by their emotions.

The experience of trauma, loss and attachment difficulties can have long-term effects on children including how they relate to others, even if new relationships are caring, safe and secure. Trauma has been associated with a number of concerning behaviours in school including lack of emotional regulation, poor planning and organisational skills, difficulties with working memory and difficulties with transitions between activities, places or objects of attention. Problems in social interactions with peers can lead to an inability for children to cope with the school environment.

Special educational needs and disabilities also have a significant impact on attainment. Looked-after children are almost four times more likely to have a special educational need than all children, and are almost nine times more likely to have an Education, Health and Care Plan than all children (6). The most common primary need in looked-after children is social, emotional and mental health. Approximately 50 per cent of secondary aged children with EHC plans have diagnosable mental health and well–being issues compared to just under 20 per cent with speech, language and communication needs and 13 per cent with moderate learning difficulties (7). This is a very different profile to children with special educational needs and disabilities who are not looked after, where approximately 12 per cent of those with EHC plans have special educational needs and disabilities as their primary need (7).

The main reasons for pupils dropping out of school involve social and emotional factors. Social and emotional aspects of learning are the underpinning qualities and skills that help individuals build resilience and manage life including recognising and managing emotions, developing concern for others, establishing positive relationships, making responsible decisions and effectively handling challenging situations. Instead of providing pupils with encouragement and interest, education can become a vicious cycle of disadvantage if children and young people are not given the chance of success. When considering factors that inhibit looked-after children to achieve educationally, they indicate that, moving home and changing school, low expectations, lack of praise from teachers, and school exclusions inhibit learning.

Attendance and exclusions

There is a direct association between school absences and poor educational attainment, which is further demonstrated statistically in the Green Paper, *Care Matters* (11). The percentage of looked-after children classified as persistent absentees has increased over a five-year period from 8.9 per cent in 2014 to 10.9 per cent in 2019 (6). Fewer absences and exclusions from school contribute to improved academic motivation, commitment to learning and a sense of school as a caring place.

Children who have been in care for 12 months or more are five times more likely to have a fixed period exclusion than all children. On a positive note the rate of fixed period and permanent exclusions for looked-after children has fallen over the last few years and is now less than the rate for all children (6). This decline in exclusion rates for looked-after children may be due to revised guidance on exclusions that was published in 2017 (7).

The gaps in attainment and life chances of children who are excluded and their peers who remain in education is considerable as only one per cent of excluded pupils go on to achieve five GCSEs. Being excluded from school is also a key factor leading to homelessness. The most common reason for school exclusion is persistent disruptive behaviour. Behaviour is symptomatic of an unrecognised or undiagnosed need. While it is important for schools to take actions to support every child to succeed in education, some children require more specialist support from other disciplines including health and social care. Working together through integration and successful collaboration with other professionals, carers and families can support the wider needs of individual children helping them progress and achieve educationally.

Child-centred education

In any school the curriculum should help pupils appreciate that personal development is essential to well-being and success. It is recognised that schools are well placed to support looked-after children develop qualities of resilience by providing them with an inclusive and enriched curriculum with teaching that scaffolds learning appropriate for each pupil. A curriculum that emphasises inclusion and discovery by starting with the child's interests and extending the child's field of enquiry is the starting point for making children feel worthwhile and for laying the foundation for successful educational processes.

Child-centred education is not a new concept and can be traced back to Rousseau in the 18th century, however, despite its long-standing history, child-centred education has always retained a central theme – that education must begin with the needs and interests of the child. Education should help all children develop the skills necessary to influence their own lives and inspire them to continue learning by providing positive experiences of school. Lessons that are finely modified to meet each child's identified needs work best where teachers are sensitive to the learning needs of all children and have a high level of expertise in creating varied learning tasks to ensure each child makes effective progress. Looked-after children report that recognition for small achievements, supportive relationships, high expectations and consistent and discreet support, so they are not made to feel different from other children, makes them feel worthy.

High expectations and achievement

Achievement is an important part of every child's development as achievement helps develop confidence and motivation for learning. Recognition of achievements is instrumental in encouraging looked-after children engage in education. Even the modest educational success can make a big difference to the lives of children in care.

Setting low expectations for pupils can be a real barrier to achievement. The looked-after system is criticised for not providing suitable goals, aspirations and expectations for children in care. For looked-after children to achieve, expectations need to be rooted in each individual child's abilities and circumstances with current achievements, the child's potential and steps required to support success, taken into account. A framework of high expectations and good teaching and learning is essential if every child is to be successful. It is important to recognise that some children have a high learning potential and require interesting, challenging and high-value tasks. Interventions and support should provide all children with the opportunity to achieve their potential and demonstrate their ability through attainment.

Rigorous target setting needs to provide children with academic, social and personal challenges. Involving children in decisions about targets and learning, particularly personal development, can build self-confidence and help children develop basic skills, such as contributing to group discussions and actively seeking support when faced with difficult tasks. Effective teaching provides children with opportunities to explore new experiences that in turn motivate their enjoyment of learning leading to a cycle of progression.

Achievement promotes feelings of pride, however, recognising achievement is not simply about carrying out activities but is also about learning gained in the process and reflection that takes place during and after activities. Recognising achievements through certificates helps with the reflection process. Certificates congratulate individuals and are an excellent motivational tool as well as being an effective way to celebrate achievements.

Stability and supportive relationships

In addition to achievements, children in the care system describe the importance of stability, supportive relationships and encouragement as elements of positive educational experiences. Stability and continuity are essential contributors to ensuring that looked-after children achieve educational success. Many of these children experience a lack of stability and security that leaves them with low self-worth and a lack of trust in adults. As teachers spend a great deal of time with the same children they are best placed to act as mentors or supportive adults for children who experienced adversity in their earlier lives. Developing positive relationships with teaching staff is important for looked-after children as it encourages them to attend school more regularly, engage enthusiastically in learning and be more responsive to participation in strategies that support constructive behavioural choices.

Looked-after children value having a mentor or friendly adult to support their educational needs and motivate them to work hard and achieve their targets. Long-term foster placements have been directly linked to educational success and higher educational achievement. Being looked after at an early stage and for a longer period of time is generally beneficial to children's educational progress: for example, with regard to care leavers who attended university, most spent five years or more in fewer than three placements. Positive expectations of others, usually carers, social workers, teachers or teaching assistants are a key factor in looked-after children believing it possible to pursue educational courses, career goals or independent living arrangements.

Schools are in an excellent position to influence the educational pathways of looked-after children as they offer a secure base in which children can function effectively both emotionally and cognitively. As a consistent and secure base, schools can provide compensatory relationships and experiences that support looked-after children manage their anxieties and develop resilience.

Motivation, resilience and new activities

Teachers' belief about children's potential is particularly powerful in building children's self-esteem and improving academic performance. There are close associations between expectations and motivations particularly intrinsic motivation where pupils like to learn because it interests them, or they recognise the value of learning. Success in non-academic school subjects such as sport, music and art as well as social success, such as being popular with other pupils, can also lead to increasing self-worth.

Being good at something is the foundation for children to build on. It is important for looked-after children to find something they are good at as this provides them with a focus and a boost to their self-esteem. Children explore new experiences when they have sufficient sense of control and self-confidence. As a way of building self-confidence children should be supported and encouraged to 'have a go' at trying new activities, even ones that are outside their comfort zone. As children become more capable in various skills their confidence increases which, in turn, develops their belief in themselves.

Informal learning and leisure activities are important facilitators in developing the resilience of looked-after and children supporting them to become well-rounded individuals. Recreational activities, including sports and hobbies, can enhance children's social skills and social networks thereby improving their self-efficacy. Hobbies are excellent tools for providing children with a focus. They allow children to wind down and enjoy themselves in a healthy and constructive way. Children require determination to pursue a hobby as giving up spare time on a regular basis to practise a musical instrument or attend a sports event needs commitment and tenacity. The willpower that comes from this dedication paves the way for success in other areas of life.

As a result of their often chaotic backgrounds looked-after children often experience social difficulties that may hinder the building of relationships. For them, the social experiences gained through participation in leisure activities can influence adjustment and buffer them from the negative effects of insecure attachments. The ability to work as a team, respect others and communicate with people of different ages and from different backgrounds is an important skill that benefits children now and along their pathway to adulthood. Interacting with others contributes towards looked-after children developing a personal identity and sense of self-worth. This helps them to take risks, solve problems and become active and vocal citizens that can look to the future with an optimistic attitude.

Summary

Drawing on children's interests and strengths has many advantages in the education system. To be successful, a child-centred model must include an understanding of the child's emotional safety. As children in care have often been exposed to various forms of maltreatment, an understanding of their needs is vital as the impact these adverse experiences may have on the child's development and ability to learn can prevent them from achieving the best outcomes in education.

Effective schools prepare children and young people to pass successfully academic assessments and the 'tests' of life because social and emotional competence and academic achievement are interwoven. A system that promotes looked-after children's emotional well-being is one in which the context and background for emotions and behaviour are explored by staff who are given the knowledge and skills they need to support children's positive mental health and well-being. A focus on emotional health and well-being in schools is recommended, with staff having access to training on the implications of maltreatment experienced by many looked-after children.

School staff are identified by looked-after children as the main determinants of their educational success. Having someone who genuinely cares for them is important to such children as they need to feel they can trust adults who will not let them down. While there are no simple answers, one of the most powerful factors in supporting them to enjoy learning and succeed personally, socially and educationally, is the building of positive relationships.

References

(1)   Millham, S., Bullock, R., Hosie, K., *et al*, *Give and Take: A Study of CSV's Project for Children in Care*. London: Community Service Volunteers, 1980.

(2) Stein, M. and Carey, K., *Leaving Care*. Oxford: Blackwell, 1986.

(3) Jackson, S. and McParlin, P., 'The education of children in care', *The Psychologist*, No. 19, 2006.

(4) Rivers, S., 'Supporting the education of looked-after children: the role of the virtual school head', *Adoption and Fostering*, 42 (2), 2018.

(5) Harland, L., 'Educational attainment of children and young people in the looked-after care system', *Community Practitioner*, 87 (11), 2014.

(6) Department for Education, *Outcomes for Children Looked After by Local Authorities in England*, 31 March 2019. London: DfE, 2020.

(7) Department for Education, *Outcomes for Children Looked After by Local Authorities in England*, 31 March 2016. London: DfE, 2017.

(8) Berridge, D., 'Educating young people in care: what have we learned?', *Children and Youth Services Review*, 34 (6), 2012.

(9) O'Higgins, A., Sebba, J. and Luke, N., *What is the Relationship Between Being in Care and the Educational Outcomes of Children?* Oxford: The REES Centre / University of Bristol, 2015.

(10) Department for Education, *Special Educational Needs in England: January 2016 SFR29/2016*. London: DfE, 2016.

(11) Department for Children, Schools and Families, *Care Matters: Transforming the Lives of Children and Young People in Care*, Green Paper, London: DCSF, 2006.

Don't Forget Us

Paper theatre gave the children a creative way of expressing their fears as their unique circumstances are overlooked when they interact with the external world.

CHAPTER 6

Attachment Theory and Children in Care

Saul Hillman and Antonella Cirasola

Introduction

Looked-after children will have invariably experienced a diverse range of adverse early life experiences (1), with 92 per cent emerging from backgrounds that involved abuse, neglect, family dysfunction or absent parenting (2). Furthermore, the subsequent experience of being removed from one's home (birth parents) and the transition to either foster or residential care poses enormous challenges for them.

Children growing up in unsafe and risky contexts are often in a hyper-vigilant state and monitor their environment carefully (3). Furthermore, they struggle both to be comforted and seek proximity, hampering their capacity to form a relationship (3). For instance, when placed in care, they might often push the foster carers away when they are upset rather than seek comfort, with the consequence that they elicit less nurturing behaviour from the foster carer (4).

There are many lenses through which fostering relationships can be understood and supported. This chapter will focus on attachment theory, one of the most dominant approaches in the conceptualisation of fostering relationships (5, 6). It will not be possible to present a complete history or thorough delineation of attachment theory. Rather, the intention is to give enough information to present how attachment theory has been applied to the context of fostering relationships.

Children in care through the lens of attachment theory

Originally developed by Bowlby (7, 8, 9), attachment theory suggests that children come into the world biologically pre-programmed to form close affectional bonds, which become a fundamental platform for the child's emerging self-concept and view of the social world. Based on ethological theory, Bowlby conceptualised human motivation to attachment in terms of a 'behavioural system' that, by eliciting and seeking protective response from the main caregiver, enhances the infant's chances for survival. Since the attachment figure serves as a secure base to explore the world, attachment theory concerns more than attachment itself, being linked to the exploratory and fear behavioural systems.

Over time, Bowlby theorised that a child would develop internal working models of the nature of their relationship with attachment figures. Internal Working Models (IWM) are internal representations of a relationship and its participants, as well as how those participants interact within that relationship (7, 8, 10, 11). These dynamic mental representations, with both cognitive and emotional components, provide 'a set of conscious and/or unconscious rules for the organisation of information relevant to attachment, and for obtaining or limiting access to that information' (12). They provide a model of others as being trustworthy; a model of the self as valuable; and a model of the self as effective when interacting with others.

Based on his work with children separated from their caregivers, Bowlby proposed that early disruptions to a child's relationship with their primary caregiver could be disruptive and detrimentally impact upon their IWMs and future relationships (7, 8, 10). Advances in attachment theory have been driven by discoveries concerning individual differences in attachment and their relative stability across time. Mary Ainsworth and her colleagues (13, 14) systematically studied differences in infants' attachment behaviours and identified three distinct styles of attachment: secure, insecure–avoidant and insecure–resistant.

Securely attached children use the attachment figure as a safe base to explore the environment with the caregiver sought for comfort or reassurance in times of distress (15). Insecure–avoidant children will demonstrate a lack of confidence in the caregiver's availability. Anxious-resistant infants show poor exploration, while exhibiting high levels of distress when separated from the caregiver and are not easily comforted by the reunion. Resistant attachment is manifested in infants whose caregivers inconsistently respond to the infant's needs and signals of distress.

Later, Mary Main suggested a fourth category of disorganised attachment where infants appeared to show no consistent strategy in seeking comfort from their caregivers (16). Disorganised–disoriented infants may exhibit a mix of avoidant and resistant behaviours and display confusion and anxiety (16, 17, 18). Attachment theorists have suggested that for these children, there exists an 'irresolvable paradox' in their IWMs, leading to the child exhibiting bizarre and disorganised attachment behaviours (19, 20, 21).

Measuring attachment

Several important approaches have focused on measuring attachment styles. this section provides an overview of the most established measures of attachment in children. The Strange Situation Procedure (SSP) (14) is an observer-based standardised measure of attachment in infants aged 9–18 months. It involves the assessment of children's responses to interactions with their caregiver, including separation, reunion, and an encounter with a stranger.

As children move beyond infancy, a less observational and behavioural approach is necessary given that the child develops the capacity to use their knowledge about a carer's availability to feel secure, even when they are not present. Here, observable attachment behaviour may be less evident and attachment representations may be more relevant. Story-stem tasks are the most commonly used tools used to investigate representations of attachment in middle childhood (The MacArthur Story Stem Battery [MSSB], (22); Attachment Story Completion Task [ASCT] (23); Manchester Child Attachment Story Task [MCAST] (24); Story Stem Assessment Profile [SSAP] (25)). One such narrative task, the SSAP, presents children with a number of different story-stem dilemmas using doll and animal figures which they are asked to respond to. The subsequent story responses are rated using a manual that allows for an assessment of attachments and relationships, without asking direct questions about the family that might cause conflict or anxiety.

Story-stem research has explored a diverse range of areas with a strong focus on attachment (26, 24, 27, 28), while they have been used extensively in looked-after populations (for example, 29, 30, 31, 32, 33, 34). Similarly, children's drawings have also been used to assess many domains including perceptions of interpersonal relationships (35, 36) and indicators of trauma and maltreatment (37). As with story stems, these are often used in adoptive and foster care populations as a measure of relationship to both self and others (31, 36, 38, 39, 40).

Beyond the latency period, older children and adolescents might respond to more direct interviews including the Child Attachment Interview (41), used in one study with this population (42), the Attachment Style Interview for Adolescents (ASI–AD, 43), the Vulnerable Attachment Style Questionnaire (VASQ, 44) and the Disturbances of Attachment Interview (DAI, 45). Such approaches, however, that involve asking direct questions whether through interview or self–report about attachment experiences (for example, Inventory and Parent and Peer Attachment (46); Relationship Problems Questionnaire (47)) have had concerns about causing too much anxiety, particularly in children with a history of negative caregiver interactions.

Attachment in looked-after children

Evidently, children's negative experiences such as abuse, neglect, and other frightening parental behaviour promote attachment problems, especially disorganized attachment (48, 49, 50, 51, 52) which can result in a paradox with parents or carers experienced as trustable, but at the same time as a possible threat or harm (18, 20, 53, 54). These contradictory and incongruent experiences make the formation of secure attachments more problematic (7, 8, 55, 56). On the one hand, a relocation into a new home brings with it loss of familiar carers, which can further impede the formation of a secure attachment (7, 8, 55, 56). On the contrary, children who develop a secure attachment with at least one stable attachment figure are more likely to have better developmental outcomes (57). Here, these ideas about relationships become internalised into internal working models and generalised to new relationships and experiences (58). Initially, they might perceive other attachment figures as repeating past experiences, thus confirming and strengthening the child's current model (28). Research on attachment relationships of children in care is inconsistent. In some studies, no differences in the rates of quality of attachment between foster children and a control or comparison group were found (32, 59, 60, 61). Due to higher levels of early relational trauma and prolonged separation from primary caregivers, children living in foster care are significantly more likely to show insecure patterns of attachment or attachment disorders (31, 32, 42, 62, 63, 64, 65, 66, 67, 68). Furthermore, studies have also reported higher rates of disorganised attachment (31, 32, 42, 66, 69, 70, 71, 72, 73).

It is important to notice that the strategies developed by children to respond to their birth parents' care may have been 'adaptive' for contexts of abuse or neglect but may create confusing signals for new foster carers (63). Not surprisingly, many foster carers report that the children they care for show confusing behaviours such as a lack of interest in or rejection of care (74). Research has shown that though they may form secure attachment relationships with their foster parents, they exhibit disinhibited attachment behaviour, making them resistant to environmental change (32, 75, 76, 77).

Overall, findings suggested that if a child experiences their caregiver as avoidant, ambivalent or antagonistic, they will have to adapt their attachment needs, which would subsequently compromise their ability to manage their emotions, thoughts and behaviours (78). If we think about a child in foster or residential care, they will have experienced relationship difficulties owing to repeated placement moves, disruptions and rejections, which results in a 'double deprivation' (79) which adds complexity to the formulation of new relationships (80, 81). A further perspective on such children emerges from other studies that suggest that though they may form secure attachment relationships with their foster parents, they can exhibit disinhibited attachment behaviour, making them resistant to environmental change (32, 75, 76, 77).

Attachment applications in foster care

Attachment theory has been one of the most dominant theories used in understanding and developing supports for fostering relationships (5, 6, 74) and has significantly contributed to professional social work (6). For example, one reason for the increasing demand for foster care placements is the assumption that permanency and consistent caregiving are necessary for children's well-being and that this cannot easily be achieved in group home or residential settings (5, 82).

One way in which attachment theory has been applied to fostering relationships is as a theoretical model for framing the psychological experiences of children living in foster care. Schofield and colleagues (3, 83) argue that children in foster care may carry IWMs from their relationships with birth parents.

Considerable interest exists in both stability and change in attachment patterns within populations of looked-after children. Promisingly, there is emerging evidence to suggest that looked-after children can develop secure attachments to their foster carers over time, despite existing insecure attachments with birth parents (84). It appears that attachment styles are, therefore, capable of change as a result of a responsive and positive foster care relationship (64). Further longitudinal studies in these populations suggest noticeable improvement or 'catch up' during the first year of placement (30, 64, 85, 86). Gabler and colleagues (64) reported an increase in attachment security during the first six months within the foster home followed by a further increase until 12 months post-placement whilst parenting style and sensitivity made a strong contribution towards the increased security (64). In a mixed-methods study (30), story-stem representations were measured at placement and then 12 months later on 19 children aged five to 10 years old and demonstrated that security ratings significantly increased whilst defensive–avoidance ones decreased. However, levels of the two negative constructs (insecurity and disorganisation) did not decrease significantly. Perhaps, this trend is very indicative of the uneven and complex trajectory that is seen, even when a child is placed in a stable and positive environment.

Such mixed trajectories can be thought about in relation to what were described as mixed attachment patterns involving multiple attachment behaviours (87). For instance, a child with past experience of a complex and traumatic family situation is likely to have developed an insecure or ambivalent attachment behaviour to cope with their early unsafe environment; however, such behaviours might no longer be 'adaptive' in a new and more stable context. This might lead to the development of new, more positive attachment behaviours, but also frequent oscillations into previous attachment patterns.

Though studies within this population have showed mixed results on the changeability of IWMs over time, it is important to notice that the methodological approaches varied including choice of measures/tools; sampling (age, size, inclusion/exclusion criteria, strategy); measurement time points; and controlling factors/variables) which are likely to have impacted the results. Overall, there is sufficient evidence that IWMs of children can change if they are placed in a safe environment, though the trajectory is often uneven with some of the more negative representations diminishing at a much slower rate.

Such trajectories of improved attachment have also been found in adoptive populations (29, 88). This might suggest that children's psychological experiences and behaviour can be transformed through appropriate parenting practices and the potential rewriting of attachment patterns (29, 89). In contrast, if people in foster care do not have the opportunity to form secure attachments, this can lead to emotional and behavioural difficulties (90, 91, 92). Stovall and Dozier (93) also found that the age at which children were placed with foster carers also played a role, with children placed with foster carers before they were 12 months old more likely to form secure attachments, potentially implying greater relevance of these theories to children coming into care at a younger age (93). However, Joseph and colleagues (84) have shown that young people who come to live with foster carers as adolescents are also able to form secure attachments to their foster carers, a finding replicated in other studies (94, 95). Several factors affected the likelihood of adolescents having secure attachments with their foster carers with adolescents who had come into care younger and lived with foster carers who had a positive and warm parenting approach most likely to form secure attachments.

Attachment theory has also been used to understand what type of care children who have experienced early adversity (for example, loss, neglect, abuse) might need from their foster carers. For instance, Schofield and Beek (3) developed a model to explain how children entering foster need support to develop secure attachments to their foster carers (3). These characteristics were found to include:

- trust in the foster carers' availability
- children's reflective functioning
- children's self-esteem
- children's family membership, and
- children's autonomy.

Attachment theory's conceptualisation of why and how children living in foster care may fail to signal their needs appropriately to new caregivers also helps inform foster carers' parenting practices (3, 83). While avoidant children may behave undemandingly or aloofly, failing to signal their need for care, ambivalent children may make constant demands, encouraging potentially intrusive caregiving styles in sensitive foster carers. Equally, children with disorganised attachment patterns may be perceived as hard to read or reach due to inconsistent signalling of needs. Even for children securely attached to birth family members, forming a new attachment with a foster carer may bring its own challenges. Schofield and colleagues emphasise the importance of foster carers recognising these patterns in the children they care for and working to interrupt these with a flexible parenting approach, avoiding the replication of previous caregiving patterns (83). Foster carers may use understandings about children's attachment patterns to know when to persist in parenting approaches that may not align with a child's cues about what they need, and when they ought to be sensitive to these cues.

Parental behaviours will undeniably play a significant part in children's attachment representations and own behaviour. Stovall and Dozier (96) found that children in care were more likely to show secure attachment behaviour with foster carers who persist in nurturing behaviours, despite children's more negative attachment behaviour (eg resistant) (96). However, findings regarding the association between sensitive caregiving and children's security of attachment are mixed. While Ponciano demonstrated higher rates of secure attachment in infants under four living with foster carers with higher maternal sensitivity (61), Cole found the opposite pattern (71). This points to the complexity of the role of sensitive parenting in foster carers and the need for further research on the topic.

Notably, to date, scarce attention has been paid to the role of foster carers' own attachment patterns in children's ability to form secure attachments to them. This is a relevant area for further research, especially given a core tenant of attachment theory (97) is the intergenerational transmission of attachment patterns. To date, findings on the topic are mixed. In line with research with children living with their birth parents, Dozier and colleagues found that infants placed with foster carers with secure attachment styles were more likely to form secure attachments to their foster carers (98). However, Caltabiano and Thorpe (99) found that carer's ability to provide high quality placements as rated by senior social workers, was not related to measurements of foster carers' attachment styles (98).

Critiques of attachment theory as a model for understanding fostering relationships

Despite attachment theory's wide application to fostering relationships, there have also been numerous critiques of this approach in a fostering context (6). For instance, some believe that attachment theory has become a master theory that ultimately has a limiting impact on our understanding of the relational worlds of children living in foster care. In particular, Smith *et al* highlight how an over-reliance on attachment theory can neglect to recognise the role of socio–cultural perspectives in children's care (5). For instance, large numbers of children living in care belong to cultures-of-origin in which typical attachment patterns may differ, and in many cultures insecure attachment is frequent (5, 100). As such, when using attachment theory, it is crucial to consider whether it is the most culturally appropriate lens through which to understand the relationships between children and their carers.

It has also been argued that attachment theory might have become so dominant in social care circles that sometimes there is little scope to consider alternate factors that may matter in the lives of children living in care or their foster carers (5). As a consequence, this can place a great deal of pressure on foster carers who are encouraged to develop attachments to the children in their care but often have these relationships broken for reasons outside of their control (101). Overall, it is important to recognise that attachment is not an isolated process but occurs in a wider context and there may be other factors in fostering relationship that may also be important to understand and account for.

Summary

This chapter has examined children in care through the lens of attachment theory and has attempted to reflect upon its theoretical and research context. Though this chapter has argued that there are other theories and models that are also applicable to comprehending this population, attachment theory remains highly useful as a way of fathoming both looked-after children's emotional and behavioural issues and the importance of stable placement. Given the vast numbers of looked-after children in the UK and the often extensive and discontinuous time they spend in care, it would be relevant for professionals and carers to understand the way in which past relational experiences impacts on their current behaviours and their relationship with their new caregivers, so that they are better prepared to provide appropriate care and meet the specific needs of these children while they find a permanent or stable home. This is especially relevant since there is sufficient evidence that there are positive and encouraging changes in internal representations of attachment during the course of a stable and safe placement. Given the important role that foster carers seem to play in their children's life, it is crucial to support them to develop positive relationships and prevent placement breakdown. Not surprisingly, over the last decade, several researchers and clinicians have developed training to support carers. Amongst those are the Reflective Fostering Programme (102, 103) and Fostering Changes. Future research should investigate if such trainings are effective in preventing placement breakdown and improving foster children attachment over time.

Contemporary attachment theory has focused on identifying those factors that may contribute to the formation of secure attachments and the mechanisms via which attachment patterns might be transferred intergenerationally from caregivers to children. Potential important mechanisms that have received significant focus in modern attachment theory work have been the role of caregiver sensitivity, mind-mindedness, mentalisation and epistemic trust (104, 105). The specific importance of these characteristics of caregivers and caregiver–child relationships also deserves further investigation.

References

(1) Morgan, K. and Baron, R., 'Challenging behaviour in looked-after young people, feelings of parental self–efficacy and psychological well-being in foster carers', *Adoption & Fostering*, 35 (1) 18–32, 2011. https://doi.org/10.1177/030857591103500104

(2) Department for Education, *Statistical First Release: Children looked after in England (including adoption)*, Department for Education, 2019.

(3) Schofield, G. and Beek, M., 'Providing a secure base: Parenting children in long-term foster family care', *Attachment & Human Development*, 7 (1) 3–26, 2005. https://doi.org/10.1080/14616730500049019

(4) Dozier, M. and Rutter, M., 'Challenges to the development of attachment relationships faced by young children in foster and adoptive care'. In J. Cassidy and P. R. Shaver (Eds), *Handbook of Attachment: Theory, Research and Clinical Applications*, New York, NY: Guilford Press, 2008.

(5) Smith, M., Cameron, C. and Reimer, D., 'From attachment to recognition for children in care', *The British Journal of Social Work*, 47 (6) 1606–1623, 2017. https://doi.org/10.1093/bjsw/bcx096

(6) White, S., Gibson, M., Wastell, D. and Walsh, P., *Reassessing Attachment Theory in Child Welfare*. Bristol: Policy Press, 2020.

(7) Bowlby, J., *Attachment and Loss: Volume 1. Attachment*. New York: Basic Books, 1969/1982.

(8) Bowlby, J., *Attachment and Loss: Volume 2. Separation: Anxiety and anger*. New York: Basic Books, 1973.

(9) Bowlby, J., *Attachment and Loss: Volume 3. Loss: Sadness and depression*. New York: Basic Books, 1980.

(10) Bowlby, J., *A Secure Base: Parent–Child Attachment and Healthy Human Development*. New York: Basic Books, 1988.

(11) Goldberg, S., *Attachment and Development* (1st edition). London: Routledge, 2000. https://doi.org/10.4324/9780203783832

(12) Main, M., Kaplan, N. and Cassidy, J., Security in infancy, childhood, and adulthood: A move to the level of representation', *Monographs of the society for research in child development*, 66–104, 1985. https://doi.org/10.2307/3333827

(13) Ainsworth, M. D. and Wittig, B. A., 'Attachment and exploratory behaviour of one-year-olds in a strange situation'. In B. M. Foss (Ed) *Determinants of Infant Behaviour* (Vol. 4). London: Methuen, 1969.

(14) Ainsworth, M. D. S., Blehar, M. C., Waters, E. and Wall, S., *Patterns of Attachment: Psychological Study of the Strange Situation*. New Jersey: Lawrence Erlbaum, 1978.

(15) Main, M. and Cassidy, J., 'Categories of response to reunion with the parent at age 6: predictable from infant attachment classifications and stable over a 1-month period', *Developmental psychology*, 24 (3) 415, 1988. https://doi.org/10.1037/0012–1649.24.3.415

(16) Main, M. and Solomon, J., 'Procedures for identifying infants as disorganized/disoriented during the Ainsworth Strange Situation', *Attachment in the Preschool Years: Theory, Research, and Intervention*, 1, 121–160, 1980.

(17) Ainsworth, M. D. and Eichberg, C. G., 'Effects of infant mother attachment of mothers' unresolved loss of an attachment figure or other traumatic experiences'. In P. Marris, J. Stevenson-Hinde and C. Parkes (Eds), *Attachment Across the Life Circle*. New York: Routledge, 1991.

(18) Hesse, E. and Main, M., 'Disorganized infant, child, and adult attachment: collapse in behavioral and attentional strategies', *Journal of the American Psychoanalytic Association*, 48 (4) 1097–1127, 2000. https://doi.org/10.1177/00030651000480041101

(19) Ensink, K., Borelli, J. L., Roy, J. et al, 'Costs of not getting to know you: Lower levels of parental reflective functioning confer risk for maternal insensitivity and insecure infant attachment', *Infancy*, 24 (2), 210–227, 2019. https://doi.org/10.1111/infa.12263

(20) Hildyard, K. L. and Wolfe, D. A., 'Child neglect: Developmental issues and outcomes', *Child Abuse & Neglect*, 26 (6–7) 679–695, 2002.

(21) Vasileva, M. and Petermann, F., 'Attachment, development, and mental health in abused and neglected preschool children in foster care: m meta-analysis', *Trauma, Violence & Abuse*, 19 (4), 443–458, 2018. https://doi.org/10.1177/1524838016669503

(22) Bretherton, I., Oppenheim, D., Buchsbaum, H., and Emde, R. N., *The MacArthur story stem battery* (MSSB). Unpublished Manual, University of Wisconsin-Madison, Madison, Wisconsin, USA, 1990.

(23) Bretherton, I., Ridgeway, D., and Cassidy, J., 'Assessing internal working models of the attachment relationship', *Attachment in the Preschool Years: Theory, Research, and Intervention*, 273, 308, 1990.

(24) Green, J., Stanley, C., Smith, V. and Goldwyn, R., 'A new method of evaluating attachment representations in young school-age children: The Manchester Child Attachment Story Task', *Attachment & Human Development*, 2 (1) 48–70, 2000. https://dol.org/10.1080/1461673003613182000

(25) Hodges, J. and Hillman, S., *Story Stem Assessment Profile (SSAP)*. Unpublished Coding Manual. London: Anna Freud Centre, 2007.

(26) Granot, D. and Mayseless, O., 'Attachment security and adjustment to school in middle childhood, *International Journal of Behavioral Development*, 25 (6) 530–541, 2001. https://doi.org/10.1080/01650250042000366

(27) Oppenheim, D. and Waters, H. S., 'Narrative processes and attachment representations: Issues of development and assessment', *Monographs of the Society for Research in Child Development*, 197–215, 1995. https://doi.org/10.2307/1166179

(28) Hodges, J., Steele, M., Hillman, S., Henderson, K. and Kaniuk, J., 'Changes in attachment representations over the first year of adoptive placement: narratives of maltreated children', *Clinical Child Psychology and Psychiatry*, 8 (3) 351–367, 2003. https://doi.org/10.1177/1359104503008003006

(29) Hillman, S., Hodges, J., Steele, M. *et al*, 'Assessing changes in the internal worlds of early-and-late-adopted children using the Story Stem Assessment Profile (SSAP)', *Adoption & Fostering*, 44 (4) 377–396, 2020a. https://doi.org/10.1177/0308575920971132

(30) Hillman, S., Villegas, C., Anderson, K. *et al*, 'Internal representations of attachment in story stems: changes in the narratives of foster care children', *Journal of Child Psychotherapy*, 2022. doi: 10.1080/0075417X.2022.2088824

(31) Pace, C. S., Guerriero, V. and Zavattini, G. C., 'Children's attachment representations: a pilot study comparing family drawing with narrative and behavioral assessments in adopted and community children', *The Arts in Psychotherapy*, 67, 101612, 2020. https://doi.org/10.1016/j.aip.2019.101612

(32) Quiroga, M. G., Hamilton-Giachritsis, C. and Fanés, M. I., 'Attachment representations and socio–emotional difficulties in alternative care: a comparison between residential, foster and family based children in Chile', *Child Abuse & Neglect*, 70, 180–189, 2017. https://doi.org/10.1016/j.chiabu.2017.05.021

(33) Román, M., Palacios, J., Moreno, C. and López, A., 'Attachment representations in internationally adopted children', *Attachment & Human Development*, 14 (6) 585–600, 2012. https://doi.org/10.1080/14616734.2012.727257

(34) Toussaint, E., Florin, A., Schneider, B. and Bacro, F., 'Les problèmes de comportement, les représentations d'attachement et le parcours de placement d'enfants relevant de la protection de l'enfance', *Neuropsychiatrie de l'Enfance et de l'Adolescence*, 66 (6) 335–343, 2018. https://doi.org/10.1016/j.neurenf.2018.07.011

(35) Burns, R. and Kaufman, S., *Actions, Styles and Symbols in Kinetic Family Drawings (K–F–D): An Interpretive Manual*. New York: Brunner/Mazel, 1972.

(36) Pace, C. S., Di Folco, S., Guerriero, V., Santona, A. andTerrone, G., 'Adoptive parenting and attachment: Association of the internal working models between adoptive mothers and their late–adopted children during adolescence', *Frontiers in Psychology*, 6, 1433, 2015. https://doi.org/10.3389/fpsyg.2015.01433

(37) Veltman, M. W. and Browne, K. D., 'The assessment of drawings from children who have been maltreated: A systematic review, *Child Abuse Review: Journal of the British Association for the Study and Prevention of Child Abuse and Neglect*, 11 (1) 19–37, 2002. https://doi.org/10.1002/car.712

(38) Betts, D. J., 'Developing a projective drawing test: experiences with the Face Stimulus Assessment (FSA)', *Art Therapy*, 20 (2), 77–82, 2003. https://doi.org/10.1080/07421656.2003.10129393

(39) Howard, A. R. H., Razuri, E. B., Call, C. D. *et al*, 'Family drawings as attachment representations in a sample of post–institutionalized adopted children', *The Arts in Psychotherapy*, 52, 63–71, 2017. https://doi.org/10.1016/j.aip.2016.09.003

(40) Katsurada, E., Tanimukai, M. and Akazawa, J., 'A study of associations among attachment patterns, maltreatment, and behavior problem in institutionalized children in Japan', *Child Abuse & Neglect*, 70, 274–282, 2017. https://doi.org/10.1016/j.chiabu.2017.06.018

(41) Shmueli-Goetz, Y., Target, M., Datta, A. and Fonagy, P., *Child attachment interview (CAI) Coding and Classification Manual. Version IV*. London: The Sub-Department of Clinical Health Psychology, University College London, 2000.

(42) Zaccagnino, M., Cussino, M., Preziosa, A. *et al*, 'Attachment representation in Institutionalized children: a preliminary study using the Child Attachment Interview', *Clinical Psychology & Psychotherapy*, 22 (2), 165–175, 2014. https://doi.org/10.1002/cpp.1882

(43) Bifulco, A., Jacobs, C., Bunn, A. *et al*, 'The Attachment Style Interview (ASI): A support–based adult assessment tool for adoption and fostering practice', *Adoption & Fostering*, 32 (3) 33–45, 2008. https://doi.org/10.1177/030857590803200306

(44) Bifulco, A., Mahon, J., Kwon, J. H. *et al*, 'The Vulnerable Attachment Style Questionnaire (VASQ): an interview-based measure of attachment styles that predict depressive disorder', *Psychological Medicine*, 33 (6) 1099–1110, 2003. https://doi.org/10.1017/s0033291703008237

(45) Smyke, A. T. and Zeanah, C. H., 'Disturbances of attachment interview', Unpublished manuscript, 1999.

(46) Armsden, G. C. and Greenberg, M. T., 'The inventory of parent and peer attachment: individual differences and their relationship to psychological well-being in adolescence', *Journal of Youth and Adolescence*, 16 (5) 427–454, 1987. https://doi.org/10.1007/bf02202939

(47) Minnis, H., Rabe–Hesketh, S. and Wolkind, S., 'Development of a brief, clinically relevant, scale for measuring attachment disorders', *International Journal of Methods in Psychiatric Research*, 11 (2) 90–98, 2002. https//doi.org/10.1002/mpr.127.

(48) Baer, J. C. and Martinez, C. D., 'Child maltreatment and insecure attachment: a meta-analysis', *Journal Of Reproductive and Infant Psychology*, 24 (3) 187–197, 2006. https://doi.org/10.1080/02646830600821231

(49) Carlson, V., Cicchetti, D., Barnett, D. and Braunwald, K. (1989) Disorganized/disoriented attachment relationships in maltreated infants. *Developmental Psychology*, 25 (4) 525. https://doi.org/10.1037/0012-1649.25.4.525

(50) Cicchetti, D., Rogosch, F. A. and Toth, S. L., 'Fostering secure attachment in infants in maltreating families through preventive interventions', *Development and Psychopathology*, 18 (3) 623–649, 2006. https://doi.org/10.1017/s0954579406060329

(51) Cyr, C., Euser, E. M., Bakermans-Kranenburg, M. J. and Van Ijzendoorn, M. H., 'Attachment security and disorganization in maltreating and high-risk families: a series of meta-analyses', *Development and Psychopathology*, 22 (1) 87–108, 2010. https://doi.org/10.1017/s0954579409990289

(52) Schuengel, C., Bakermans-Kranenburg, M. J. and Van IJzendoorn, M. H., 'Frightening maternal behavior linking unresolved loss and disorganized infant attachment', *Journal of Consulting and Clinical Psychology*, 67 (1) 54, 1999. https://doi.org/10.1037/0022-006x.67.1.54

(53) Cicchetti, D., *Developmental Psychopathology*, Chichester: John Wiley & Sons, Inc, 2010. https://doi.org/10.1002/9780470880166.hlsd002014

(54) Hesse, E. and Main, M., 'Frightened, threatening, and dissociative parental behavior in low-risk samples: Description, discussion, and interpretations', *Development and Psychopathology*, 18 (2) 309–343, 2006. https://doi.org/10.1017/s0954579406060172

(55) Juffer, F., Palacios, J., Le Mare, L., Sonuga-Barke, E. J. *et al*, 'II. Development of adopted children with histories of early adversity', *Monographs of the Society for Research in Child Development*, 76 (4) 31–61, 2011. https://doi.org/10.1111/j.1540-5834.2011.00627.x

(56) Stovall, K. C. and Dozier, M., 'Infants in foster care: an attachment theory perspective', *Adoption Quarterly*, 2 (1) 55–88, 1998. https://doi.org/10.1300/j145v02n01_05

(57) Van IJzendoorn, M. H. and Bakermans-Kranenburg, M. J., The Distribution of Adult Attachment Representations in Clinical Groups: A Meta–analytic Search for Patterns of Attachment in 105 AAI studies. Unpublished Document, 2008.

(58) Kobak, R., Zajac, K., Herres, J. and Krauthamer Ewing, E. S., 'Attachment based treatments for adolescents: the secure cycle as a framework for assessment, treatment and evaluation', *Attachment & Human Development*, 17 (2) 220–239, 2015. https://doi.org/10.1080/14616734.2015.1006388

(59) Jacobsen, H., Ivarsson, T., Wentzel-Larsen, T. *et al*, 'Attachment security in young foster children: continuity from 2 to 3 years of age', *Attachment & Human Development*, 16 (1) 42–57, 2014. https://doi.org/10.1080/14616734.2013.850102

(60) Oosterman, M. and Schuengel, C., 'Attachment in foster children associated with caregivers' sensitivity and behavioral problems', *Infant Mental Health Journal: Official Publication of the World Association for Infant Mental Health*, 29 (6) 609–623, 2008. https://doi.org/10.1002/imhj.20198

(61) Ponciano, L., 'Attachment in foster care: the role of maternal sensitivity, adoption, and foster mother experience', *Child and Adolescent Social Work Journal*, 27 (2) 97–114, 2010. https://doi.org/10.1007/s10560–010–0192–y

(62) Ballús, E., Casas, M., Urrutia, E. and Pérez–Testor, C., 'Attachment representations in international adolescent adoptees in Spain, over 8 to 17 years of placement', *International Social Work*, 62 (6) 1507–1521, 2019. https://doi.org/10.1177/0020872819878484

(63) Howe, D. and Fearnley, S., 'Disorders of attachment in adopted and fostered children: recognition and treatment', *Clinical Child Psychology and Psychiatry*, 8 (3) 369–387, 2013. https://doi.org/10.1177/1359104503008003007

(64) Gabler, S., Bovenschen, I., Lang, K. *et al*, 'Foster children's attachment security and behavior problems in the first six months of placement: associations with foster parents' stress and sensitivity', *Attachment & Human Development*, 16 (5) 479–498, 2014. https://doi.org/10.1080/14616734.2014.911757

(65) Goemans, A., van Geel, M. and Vedder, P., 'Over three decades of longitudinal research on the development of foster children: a meta-analysis', *Child Abuse & Neglect*, 42, 121–134, 2015. https://doi.org/10.1016/j.chiabu.2015.02.003

(66) Hillman, S., Cross, R., and Anderson, K., 'Exploring attachment and internal representations in looked-after children', *Frontiers in Psychology*, 11, 2020b. https://doi.org/10.3389/fpsyg.2020.00464

(67) Minnis, H., Everett, K., Pelosi, A. J. *et al*, 'Children in foster care: mental health, service use and costs', *European Child & Adolescent Psychiatry*, 15 (2) 63–70, 2006. https://doi.org/10.1007/s00787-006-0452-8

(68) Takayama, J. I., Wolfe, E. and Coulter, K. P., 'Relationship between reason for placement and medical findings among children in foster care', *Pediatrics*, 101 (2) 201–20, 1998. https://doi.org/10.1542/peds.101.2.201

(69) Bifulco, A., Jacobs, C., Ilan–Clarke, Y. *et al*, 'Adolescent attachment style in residential care: the attachment style interview and vulnerable attachment style questionnaire', *British Journal of Social Work*, 47 (7) 1870–1883, 2017.

(70) Bovenschen, I., Lang, K., Zimmermann, J. *et al*, 'Foster children's attachment behavior and representation: influence of children's pre-placement experiences and foster caregiver's sensitivity'. *Child Abuse & Neglect*, 51, 323–335, 2016. https://doi.org/10.1016/j.chiabu.2015.08.016

(71) Cole, S. A., 'Building secure relationships: Attachment in kin and unrelated foster caregiver–infant relationships', *Families in Society*, 87 (4) 497–508, 2006. https://doi.org/10.1606/1044-3894.3565

(72) Dozier, M., Stoval, K. C., Albus, K. E. and Bates, B., 'Attachment for infants in foster care: The role of caregiver state of mind', *Child Development*, 72 (5) 1467–1477, 2001. https://doi.org/10.1111/1467-8624.00360

(73) Fearon, R. P., Bakermans-Kranenburg, M. J., Van IJzendoorn, M. H. *et al*, 'The significance of insecure attachment and disorganization in the development of children's externalizing behavior: a meta-analytic study', *Child Development*, 81 (2) 435–456, 2010. https://doi.org/10.1111/j.1467-8624.2009.01405.x

(74) Steele, M., The 'added value' of attachment theory and research for clinical work in adoption and foster care. In J. Kenrick, C. Lindsey, C. and L. Tollemache, *Therapeutic Approaches to Fostering, Adoption and Kinship Care*. London: Routledge, 2006. https://doi.org/10.4324/9780429473395-5

(75) Chisholm, K., 'A three-year follow-up of attachment and indiscriminate friendliness in children adopted from Romanian orphanages', *Child Development*, 69 (4) 1092–1106, 1998. https://doi.org/10.1111/j.1467–8624.1998.tb06162.x

(76) O'Connor, T. G., Marvin, R. S., Rutter, M. *et al*, English and Romanian Adoptees Study Team: Child parent attachment following early institutional deprivation. *Dev. and Psychopathol.*, 15 (1) 19–38, Winter, 2003. https://doi.org/10.1017/s0954579403000026

(77) Zimmermann, J., *Symptoms of Disordered Attachment in High-Risk Populations: Prevalence, Risk Factors, and Prevention (doctoral dissertation)*. Friedrich-Alexander-Universität Erlangen-Nürnberg (FAU), 2015.

(78) Howe, D., 'Developmental attachment psychotherapy with fostered and adopted children', *Child Adolescent Mental Health*, 11 (3) 128–134, 2006. https://doi.org/10.1111/j.1475-3588.2006.00393.x

(79) Henry, G., 'Doubly deprived', *Journal of Child Psychotherapy*, 3 (4) 15–28, 1974. https://doi.org/10.1080/00754177708257300

(80) Main, M. and George, C., 'Responses of abused and disadvantaged toddlers to distress in age mates: A study in the day care setting',

Developmental Psychology, 21 (3) 407, 1985.
https://doi.org/10.1037/0012-1649.21.3.407

(81) Waldinger, R. J., Toth, S. L. and Gerber, A., 'Maltreatment and internal representations of relationships: core relationship themes in the narratives of abused and neglected preschoolers', *Social Development*, 10 (1) 41–58, 2001. https://doi.org/10.1111/1467-9507.00147

(82) Nowacki, K. and Schoelmerich, A., 'Growing up in foster families or institutions: attachment representation and psychological adjustment of young adults', *Attachment & Human Development*, 12 (6) 551–566, 2010. https://doi.org/10.1080/14616734.2010.504547

(83) Schofield, G., Beek, M., Sargent, K. and Thoburn, J., *Growing Up in Foster Care*. London: British Association for Adoption and Fostering, 2000.

(84) Joseph, M. A., O'Connor, T. G., Briskman, J. A. *et al*, 'The formation of secure new attachments by children who were maltreated: An observational study of adolescents in foster care', *Development and Psychopathology*, 26 (1) 67–80, 2013.
https://doi.org/10.1017/s0954579413000540

(85) Dallos, R., Morgan-West, K. and Denman, K., 'Changes in attachment representations for young people in long-term therapeutic foster care', *Clinical Child Psychology and Psychiatry*, 20 (4) 657–676, 2015.
https://doi.org/10.1177/1359104514543956

(86) Lang, K., Bovenschen, I., Gabler, S. *et al,* 'Foster children's attachment security in the first year after placement: a longitudinal study of predictors', *Early Childhood Research Quarterly*, 36, 269–280, 2016.
https://doi.org/10.1016/j.ecresq.2015.12.019

(87) Crittenden, P. M., 'Raising parents: attachment', *Parenting and Child Safety*, 2008. https://doi.org/10.4324/9780203069776

(88) Van den Dries, L., Juffer, F., Van IJzendoorn, M. H. and Bakermans-Kranenburg, M. J., 'Fostering security? a meta–analysis of attachment in adopted children', *Children and Youth Services Review*, 31 (3) 410–421, 2009. https://doi.org/10.1016/j.childyouth.2008.09.008

(89) Barone, L. and Lionetti, F., 'Attachment and emotional understanding: a study on late-adopted pre-schoolers and their parents', *Child Care, Health and Development*, 38 (5) 690–696, 2012.
https://doi.org/10.1080/14616734.2012.691653

(90) Luke, N. and Coyne, S. M., 'Fostering self-esteem: exploring adult recollections on the influence of foster parents', *Child & Family Social Work*, 13 (4) 402–410, 2008. https://doi.org/10.1111/j.1365-2206.2008.00565.x

(91) Richardson, J. and Lelliott, P., 'Mental health of looked-after children', *Advances in Psychiatric Treatment*, 9 (4) 249–256, 2003.
https://doi.org/10.1192/apt.9.4.249.

(92) Lasson, V., 'Children's identity', *Child & Youth Care Forum*, 31, 177–182. 2002. https://doi.org/10.1023/A:1016052405807

(93) Stovall, K.C. and Dozier, M., 'Forming attachments in foster care: Infant attachment behaviors during the first 2 months of placement', *Development and Psychopathology*, 16 (2) 253–271, 2004. https://doi.org/10.1017/s0954579404044505

(94) Barber, J. and Delfabbro, P., 'Children's adjustment to long–term foster care', *Children and Youth Services Review*, 27 (3) 329–340, 2005. https://doi.org/10.1016/j.childyouth.2004.10.010

(95) Fernandez, E., 'Children's well-being in care: Evidence from a longitudinal study of outcomes', *Children and Youth Services Review*, 31 (10) 1092–1100, 2009. https://doi.org/10.1016/j.childyouth.2009.07.010

(96) Stovall, K. C. and Dozier, M., 'The development of attachment in new relationships: single subject analyses for 10 foster infants', *Development and Psychopathology*, 12 (2) 133–156, 2000. https://doi.org/10.1017/s0954579400002029

(97) Walker, J. (2008) 'The use of attachment theory in adoption and fostering', *Adoption & Fostering*, 32 (1) 49–57. https://doi.org/10.1177/030857590803200107

(98) Dozier, M., Albus, K., Fisher, P. A. and Sepulveda, S., 'Interventions for foster parents: implications for developmental theory', *Development and Psychopathology*, 14 (4) 843–860, 2002. https://doi.org/10.1017/s0954579402004091

(99) Caltabiano, M. L. and Thorpe, R., 'Attachment style of foster carers and caregiving role performance', *Childcare in Practice*, 13 (2) 137–148, 2007. https://doi.org/10.1080/13575270701201201

(100) Burman, E., *Deconstructing Developmental Psychology* (2nd edition). London: Routledge, 2008.

(101) Pickin, L., Brunsden, V. and Hill, R., 'Exploring the emotional experiences of foster carers using the photovoice technique', *Adoption & Fostering*, 35 (2) 61–75, 2011. https://doi.org/10.1177/030857591103500207

(102) Redfern, S., Wood, S., Lassri, D. *et al*, 'The Reflective Fostering Programme: background and development of a new approach', *Adoption & Fostering*, 42 (3) 234–248, 2018. https://doi.org/10.1177/0308575918790434

(103) Midgley, N., Sprecher, E. A., Cirasola, A. *et al*, 'The reflective fostering programme: evaluating the intervention co–delivered by social work professionals and foster carers', *Journal of Children's Services*, 16 (2) 159–174, 2021. https://doi.org/10.1108/jcs-11-2020-0074

(104) Fishburn, S., Meins, E., Greenhow, S. *et al*, 'Mind-mindedness in parents of looked-after children', *Developmental Psychology*, 53 (10) 1954–1965, 2017. https://doi.org/10.1037/dev0000304

(105) Fonagy, P. and Campbell, C., 'Mentalizing, attachment and epistemic trust: how psychotherapy can promote resilience', *Psychiatria Hungarica: A Magyar Pszichiatriai Tarsasag Tudomanyos Folyoirata*, 32 (3) 283–287, 2017. https://pubmed.ncbi.nlm.nih.gov/29135441/

CHAPTER 7

Attachment in Looked-After Children: The Neuro-Scientific Evidence

Paula Oliveira

Introduction

Attachment-relevant brain imaging research with children exposed to adverse early care aims to understand whether and how such experiences have measurable effects on the brain, underpinning their poor social and behavioural outcomes. Evidence compellingly shows that early exposure to adverse or disadvantaged environments, such as institutionalisation or maltreatment, negatively affects the individual's neuro-development (1, 2, 3). Yet, studies directly investigating the neural substrates of attachment in looked-after children are lacking. Therefore, this chapter draws on different streams of literature to compile the evidence, focusing on children who are or have been looked after, but also establishing parallels with evidence from child maltreatment when relevant. First, I summarise the key general brain structural and functional findings. Then, I review the neuro-scientific evidence that is more directly relevant for understanding these children's socio-emotional development. In the last section I discuss the smaller set of studies on attachment.

Brain development in children who are looked-after

Neuro-scientific studies have documented differences in brain structure (that is, anatomy) as well as function in children placed in out of home care. It is important to note that most of this research has assessed children exposed to particularly deprived settings, characterised by lack of individualised and consistent caregiving from institutions in Eastern Europe and, less often, from Asia. However, to obtain a clearer picture from the existing evidence it is also necessary to look at the larger body of work with children who have experienced (several different types of) maltreatment.

Anatomical studies look at grey matter, which consists primarily of neuronal cell bodies, and white matter tracts connecting different cortical and/or subcortical structures. Magnetic resonance imaging (MRI) results show that institutionally reared children, when compared to those of the same age raised continuously in their birth families, have smaller volumes of both white and grey matter (4, 5), and altered structural integrity of white matter (6). In the Bucharest Early Intervention Project (BEIP), where children living in Romanian institutions were randomly assigned (between seven and 33 months of age) to remain at the institution or move to high-quality foster homes, those who moved to foster care showed an encouraging recovery in white matter volume and integrity. However, volume of grey matter showed a similar reduction to that of children who remained institutionalised. Similarly, reduced cortical grey and white matter volumes have been reported in children exposed to maltreatment (compared to non-maltreated), with important differences remaining even after controlling for their overall smaller brain size (7,8). Nevertheless, volume reductions do not seem to be distributed evenly across the brain, therefore many studies have looked at specific regions, particularly focusing on those that are known to be highly sensitive to early stress.

There is a relatively abundant literature documenting regional differences between children exposed to early caregiving adversity (mainly maltreatment) and controls, with effects predominantly reported in the emotion regulation circuitry – involving areas of the prefrontal cortex and the amygdala, as well as connectivity between them. The executive role in this circuitry is performed by the prefrontal cortex, which is crucially involved in higher-order functions such as cognitive control and emotional regulation. In some prefrontal areas, including the orbitofrontal cortex, reduced grey matter volume, blood flow and cortical thickness have been described in institutionally reared children (9,10). Similar reductions have been documented in children exposed to maltreatment (11–13).

The amygdala is a limbic structure that has received particular attention because it is critically involved in emotional processing and threat detection and is also very susceptible to the early environment. While increased amygdala volume has been documented in samples who were maltreated or institutionally reared earlier in life, usually assessed during childhood, the opposite finding of reduced volume has been reported in studies with adolescents and adults (4,14,15). This pattern suggests effects of timing of exposure and of assessment, whereby an initial stress-induced hypertrophy and hyperactivity of amygdala neurons eventually lead to neuronal atrophy or cell death by adulthood (15,16). Longitudinal evidence from post-institutionalised youth internationally adopted into the United States, provides support to this developmental trajectory of the amygdala in the context of early caregiving adversity, with larger volumes observed before 6.5 years of age, but smaller volumes from 11 onwards (17). In addition to volume differences, there are indications of alterations in network connectivity involving the amygdala, in children who experienced early adversity; yet there is preliminary evidence that the type of adversity, abuse or neglect, may lead to alterations in distinct specific regions (18).

Alterations in several fibre tracts have also been associated with adverse caregiving experiences. I will focus on the corpus callosum, which is the largest white matter tract in the brain, and key for inter-hemispheric communication (reductions in its thickness have been implicated, for example, in ADHD). Findings consistently show reduced volume and integrity of the corpus callosum in institutionally reared children (5,6), as well as in children who experienced maltreatment, including neglect (7,8,19). As seen earlier regarding recovery in white matter more generally, findings from the BEIP suggest some capacity for recovery in corpus callosum volume for children randomised to high-quality foster care, when compared to their peers who remained institutionalised (5).

Remarkably consistent with the anatomical literature just reviewed, is the electrophysiological evidence from institutionally reared children. This is research employing electroencephalography (EEG), or the related technique of event-related potentials (ERP), which measure the electrical activity of the brain via electrodes placed on the scalp. Reports are accumulating of reduced EEG power and reduced activation amongst institutionally reared children.

Findings from two different samples (20–23) indicate that children reared in institutions display higher power in low-frequency (theta) and lower power in mid- to high-frequency (alpha and beta) bands, compared to those peers who had never been institutionalised – with such a pattern documented from the toddler years up until 16 years of age. Moreover, foster children from the BEIP experiencing more caregiving disruptions also showed this pattern, identical to those who remained institutionalised (22).

The concentration of power in lower frequencies signals either abnormalities or a delay in normal brain maturation, and has been interpreted as neural hypoactivation likely resulting from the lack of stimulation from stable and responsive caregivers (20,21). Interestingly, the association between institutional care and reduced EEG alpha-power in the BEIP sample could be partly explained by the mediating role of smaller cortical white matter volume in the children who remained institutionalised (5). Therefore, it is plausible that institutional rearing has an impact in shaping brain anatomy in ways that alter neural activity. Encouragingly, the intervention effects of the foster care placement were seen, particularly for children removed from the institution before 24 months of age, whose alpha power at age eight was comparable to that of children who had never been institutionalised. This suggests that the continuous experience of high-quality foster care was able to mitigate, to some extent, the deleterious effects of deprivation, with important timing effects—particularly for alpha power, which has been associated with attention and alertness (24). Intervention findings consistent with these have been reported for children at risk for maltreatment living with their families, with those receiving an attachment-based intervention showing increases in high frequency power years later (25).

In addition to the overall reduction in EEG power, there is evidence of atypical patterns of hemispheric asymmetry associated with adverse rearing. The most compelling evidence comes from the BEIP study, where institutionalised children developed an atypical trajectory of hemispheric asymmetry, with a prolonged period of increased right hemisphere activation (until 42 months of age) and a blunted rebound in left frontal activation, meaning that by 8 years of age they had greater activity in the right than the left hemisphere, when compared to children who had never been institutionalised (and those who were placed in foster–care at earlier ages). A right alpha power asymmetry has also been reported in toddlers in foster care in the United States and in maltreated children (26,27). This common asymmetry pattern can be seen in light of the literature associating right-hemisphere dominance with withdrawal behaviour and negative emotionality (28), and a potential explanation for the increased rates of emotional and behavioural problems following early adversity – however, this association has so far been inconsistent (26).

In summary, neuro-imaging findings from children exposed to institutional rearing or maltreatment present a picture of reduced volume in stress-sensitive brain structures and reduced brain electrical activity, which seem to result from their negative early caregiving experiences and, especially, from lack of expected environmental input which the nervous system requires for typical development to unfold. Nevertheless, evidence points to the crucial intervention potential of improving caregiving to alter children's developmental trajectories.

Neuroscientific research of socio-emotional development in looked-after children

Studies of adverse early care using functional MRI (fMRI, which measures brain activation indirectly by detecting increased demand in blood oxygenation) have mainly focused on a few key regions critically involved in reward and threat processing, which are relevant for understanding social and attachment behaviour and the development of psychopathology. Overall, adverse early experiences have been linked to reduced reward and increased threat-related activation.

Research with institutionally reared children has documented a reduced activation in a region critically involved in reward processing, the ventral striatum, during reward anticipation and in response to positive cues (29,30). This is consistent with findings from youth and adults with histories of maltreatment (31,32), supporting the link between early adversity and disturbances of the reward circuit.

Studies of threat detection and regulation typically measure amygdala activation while participants visualise emotional stimuli, such as faces posing different emotional expressions. Such research has described increased amygdala activation in children adopted from care (33,34). This goes in line with evidence from individuals exposed to child maltreatment, who show increased amygdala reactivity (35,36) and difficulties in discriminating threat from safety cues during fear conditioning (37). Unsurprisingly, this increased amygdala activation is accompanied by decreased activation in regions supporting cognitive control (34,36). Increased amygdala reactivity has been hypothesised to serve an adaptive function in maltreated individuals, in allowing enhanced capacity for detecting threatening stimuli (37), even if it may lead to later difficulties, including psychopathology (36).

Another technique to analyse brain function is ERP, which measures the peaks in individuals' neural responses to the presentation of stimuli during the EEG recording. ERP research with institutionalised children often employs face stimuli, due to the relevance of faces for socio–emotional development and the hypothesised atypical exposure to faces in children raised by multiple, rotating caregivers. In a series of ERP studies with the BEIP sample, children's neural responses were recorded while they viewed pictures of their caregiver (the mother for children brought up in families) and that of a stranger. When children were seven to 32 months-old (38), and again at 30 and 42 months (39), there were marked group differences in amplitude of children's neural responses. Namely, institutionalised children showed decreased amplitudes in ERP components involved in face processing, particularly the P1 component which indexes early and low-level feature processing of visual stimuli. For children randomised to foster care, amplitudes in this component were intermediate, between the other two groups, suggesting that hypoactivation shows signs of amelioration following placement in high-quality foster care. Nevertheless, all groups of children were able to discriminate, at the neural level, the caregiver from the stranger's face, indicating that that ability was preserved even in the institutionalised group. These findings were partially replicated in a sample of pre-schoolers in foster care in Germany, who showed reduced amplitudes not in the P1 but in the component that occurs immediately after, the N170, which is a marker of more elaborate face-sensitive perceptual processes, when compared to home-reared controls (40). Therefore, blunted neural responses are observed in children exposed to different levels of deprivation, with both institutional and foster care associated with some alterations in face familiarity processing.

Neuroscientific research of attachment in looked-after children

A small number of studies has focused on attachment outcomes alongside employing neuroimaging methods. I first review those assessing children for inhibited (reactive) attachment disorder (RAD) or disinhibited social engagement symptoms.

Research using different methodologies provides initial evidence of the neural substrates of disordered attachment/social behaviour. The first included post-institutionalised adoptees, whose pattern of EEG power distribution described earlier (i.e. concentration in lower frequencies), measured at 18 months, predicted their display of socially disinhibited behaviour at 36 months (20). The second used fMRI with post-institutionalised adopted youth, who showed reduced differentiation in amygdala activation between the mother's and a stranger's face (compared to controls), which correlated with their disinhibited behaviour; also, these effects were particularly prominent in children who were adopted later in life, suggesting effects of timing of removal from institutional care (41). Consistent with both these studies is one with Portuguese institutionalised pre-schoolers, documenting smaller ERP amplitudes in the P1 component (in response to viewing caregivers' and strangers' faces) amongst those with disinhibited or inhibited attachment behaviour, when compared to their institutionalised peers without either of these symptom clusters (42). Moreover, children presenting disinhibited social behaviour did not differentiate the caregiver's from the stranger's face in any of the measured ERP components, consistent with their phenotype.

Providing novel insight into brain alterations associated with RAD, is evidence from previously maltreated youth with this diagnosis, living in a child welfare facility in Japan. These youth showed alterations in white matter, particularly in the structure of the corpus callosum and pathways that are important for emotion regulation (43)—alterations that, as we have seen, are associated with being looked-after more generally. The same team also reported reduced striatum activity in youth with RAD, during a monetary reward task (32), therefore extending findings reviewed above of the general impact of maltreatment and institutional rearing on the reward circuit. Collectively, these investigations are beginning to link institutionalised children's neural profiles with their behavioural outcomes, shedding light into the nuances of individual variation.

Now I turn to two studies linking neural correlates with attachment security among children in care.

In another piece of work with the BEIP sample (44), alpha power at eight years of age moderated the relation between children's attachment security to the primary caregiver (at 42 months) and later social skills, among all children who experienced institutionalisation. Specifically, only for children with higher alpha power, did a greater attachment security significantly predict better social skills. The second study, already mentioned, assessed children in foster care in Germany (40). In addition to the group differences we have seen, it also found that variation in attachment security played a role in children's face-familiarity processing, with insecurely attached children showing a reduced N170 component compared to secure ones. Even if preliminary, this evidence may be interpreted as increased face expertise in secure children, beyond the experience of foster care, potentially allowed by contingent social interactions within an adequately stimulating social environment provided by their caregiver (40).

To conclude, brain alterations observed in institutionally reared children, such as EEG hypoactivation and blunted ERP components, are associated with poor socio-emotional outcomes, offering tentative explanations for why some children manifest problems while others do not. The establishment of secure attachment relationships appears to buffer the negative impact of adversity on these neural systems.

Summary

This chapter provides a brief, and necessarily limited overview of the neuroscientific research that is relevant for our understanding of attachment in looked-after children. Children who have experienced early caregiving adversity show widespread neural alterations in both brain structure and function, which may result from a protective adaptation to their circumstances and/or damage to developing systems that are very sensitive to insults from the environment. These alterations are likely to partly underlie their increased rates of socioemotional and behavioural difficulties. Evidence on plasticity is scant, but there are encouraging examples of children's capacity for recovery and resilience.

An important limitation of this work is the confounding overlap and lack of differentiation between the multiple adverse caregiving experiences each child has been exposed to. At the most basic level these experiences may be differentiated in ones resulting in deprivation or threat, but often children are exposed to different combinations of maltreatment, relationship disruptions and suboptimal caregiving, which most studies are not able to account for.

Nevertheless, children in these studies were all exposed to major adverse caregiving experiences, which have in common well documented negative effects, both in terms of socio-emotional outcomes and neurodevelopment (45). Yet, clear differences also exist in the adverse outcomes associated with abuse or neglect and institutional or foster rearing (46), which must be kept in mind, and direct comparisons between samples will always be uncertain until further rigorous research has been undertaken.

References

(1) Pechtel, P. and Pizzagalli, D.A., 'Effects of early life stress on cognitive and affective function: an integrated review of human literature'. *Psychopharmacology*, 214 (1) 55–70, 2011

(2) Rutter, M., 'Achievements and challenges in the biology of environmental effects', *Proceedings of the National Academy of Sciences*, 109, 17149–53, 2012.

(3) Tomalski, P. and Johnson, M.H., 'The effects of early adversity on the adult and developing brain', *Current Opinion in Psychiatry*, 23 (3) 233–8, 2010.

(4)   Mehta, M.A., Golembo, N.I., Nosarti, C. *et al*, 'Amygdala, hippocampal and corpus callosum size following severe early institutional deprivation: the English and Romanian Adoptees study pilot', *Journal of Child Psychology and Psychiatry*, 50 (8) 943–51, 2009.

(5)   Sheridan, M.A., Fox, N.A, Zeanah, C.H. *et al*, 'Variation in neural development as a result of exposure to institutionalization early in childhood', *Proceedings of the National Academy of Sciences*, 109 (32) 12927–32, 2012.

(6)   Bick, J., Zhu, T., Stamoulis, C. *et al*, 'Effect of early institutionalization and foster care on longterm white matter development: a randomized clinical trial', *JAMA Pediatr*, 169 (3) 211–9, 2015.

(7)   De Bellis, M.D., Keshavan, M.S, Shifflett, H. *et al*, 'Brain structures in pediatric maltreatment-related post traumatic stress disorder: a sociodemographically matched study', *Biological Psychiatry*, 52 (11) 1066–78, 2002.

(8)   De Bellis, M.D., Keshavan, M.S., Clark, D.B. *et al*, 'Developmental traumatology part II: brain development', *Biological Psychiatry*, 45 (10) 1271–84, 1999.

(9)   Chugani, H.T., Behen, M.E., Muzik, O. *et al*, 'Local brain functional activity following early deprivation: a study of postinstitutionalized Romanian orphans', *NeuroImage*, 14 (6) 1290–301, 2001.

(10)   McLaughlin, K.A., Sheridan, M.A., Winter, W. *et al*, 'Widespread reductions in cortical thickness following severe early-life deprivation: a neurodevelopmental pathway to Attention–eficit/Hyperactivity Disorder', *Biological Psychiatry*, 76 (8) 629–38, 2014.

(11)   De Brito, S.A., Viding, E., Sebastian, C.L. *et al*, 'Reduced orbitofrontal and temporal grey matter in a community sample of maltreated children: reduced in maltreated children grey matter', *Journal of Child Psychology and Psychiatry*, 54 (1) 105–12, 2013.

(12)   Hanson, J.L., Chung, M.K., Avants, B.B. *et al*, 'Early stress is associated with alterations in the orbitofrontal cortex: a tensor-based morphometry investigation of brain structure and behavioral risk', *Journal of Neuroscience*, 30 (22) 7466–72, 2010.

(13)   Fujisawa, T.X., Nishitani, S., Takiguchi, S. *et al*, 'Oxytocin receptor DNA methylation and alterations of brain volumes in maltreated children', *Neuropsychopharmacol*, 44 (12) 2045–53, 2019.

(14)   Tottenham, N., Hare, T.A., Quinn, B.T. *et al*, 'Prolonged institutional rearing is associated with atypically large amygdala volume and difficulties in emotion regulation: previous institutionalization', *Developmental Science*, 13 (1) 46–61, 2010.

(15)   Tottenham, N. and Sheridan, M.A., 'A review of adversity, the amygdala and the hippocampus: A consideration of developmental timing', *Front Hum Neurosci*, 2009.

(16) Teicher, M.H. and Samson, J.A., 'Annual Research Review: Enduring neurobiological effects of childhood abuse and neglect', *J Child Psychol Psychiatr*, 57 (3) 241–66, 2016.

(17) Van Tieghem, M., Korom, M., Flannery, J. *et al*, 'Longitudinal changes in amygdala, hippocampus and cortisol development following early caregiving adversity', *Developmental Cognitive Neuroscience*, 48, 100916, 2021.

(18) Cheng, T.W., Mills, K.L., Miranda Dominguez, O. *et al*, 'Characterizing the impact of adversity, abuse, and neglect on adolescent amygdala resting-state functional connectivity', *Developmental Cognitive Neuroscience*, 47, 100894, 2021.

(19) Teicher, M.H., Dumont, N.L., Ito, Y. *et al*, 'Childhood neglect is associated with reduced corpus callosum area', *Biological Psychiatry*, 56 (2) 80–5, 2004.

(20) Tarullo, A.R., Garvin, M.C. and Gunnar, M.R., 'Atypical EEG power correlates with indiscriminately friendly behavior in internationally adopted children', *Developmental Psychology*, 47 (2) 417–31, 2011.

(21) Marshall, P.J., Fox, N.A. and Group, B.C., 'A comparison of the electroencephalogram between institutionalized and community children in Romania', *Journal of Cognitive Neuroscience*, 16 (8) 1327–38, 2004.

(22) Debnath, R., Tang, A., Zeanah, C.H. *et al*, 'The long-term effects of institutional rearing, foster care intervention and disruptions in care on brain electrical activity in adolescence', *Dev Sci.* 23 (1), 2020.

(23) Vanderwert, R.E., Marshall, P.J., Nelson, C.A. *et al*, 'Timing of intervention affects brain electrical activity in children exposed to severe psychosocial neglect', *PLoS ONE*, 5 (7) e11415, 2010.

(24) Marshall, P.J., Bar-Haim, Y. and Fox, N.A., 'Development of the EEG from 5 months to 4 years of age', *Clinical Neurophysiology*, 113 (8) 1199–208, 2002.

(25) Bick, J., Palmwood, E.N., Zajac, L. *et al*, 'Early parenting intervention and adverse family environments affect neural function in middle childhood', *Biol Psychiatry*, 85 (4) 326–35, 2019.

(26) Blaisdell, K.N., Barker, T.V., Giuliano, R.J. and Fisher P.A., 'Alpha electroencephalogram (EEG) asymmetry among toddlers in foster care', *Dev Psychopathol*, 32 (5) 1743–53, 2020.

(27) Curtis, W.J. and Cicchetti, D., 'Emotion and resilience: A multilevel investigation of hemispheric electroencephalogram asymmetry and emotion regulation in maltreated and non-maltreated children', *Dev Psychopathol*, 19 (3) 811–40, 2007.

(28) Davidson, R.J., 'Anterior cerebral asymmetry and the nature of emotion', *Brain Cogn*, 20 (1) 125–51, 1992.

(29) Mehta, M.A., Gore-Langton, E., Golembo, N. *et al*, 'Hyporesponsive reward anticipation in the basal ganglia following severe institutional deprivation early in life', *Journal of Cognitive Neuroscience*, 22 (10) 2316–25, 2010.

(30) Goff, B., Gee, D.G., Telzer, E.H. *et al*. 'Reduced nucleus accumbens reactivity and adolescent depression following early-life stress', *Neuroscience*, 249, 129–38, 2013.

(31) Dillon, D.G., Holmes, A.J., Birk, J.L., 'Childhood adversity is associated with left basal ganglia dysfunction during reward anticipation in adulthood', *Biological Psychiatry*, 66 (3) 206–13, 2009.

(32) Takiguchi, S., Fujisawa, T.X., Mizushima, S. *et al*, 'Ventral striatum dysfunction in children and adolescents with reactive attachment disorder: functional MRI study', *BJPsych Open*, 1 (2) 121–8, 2015.

(33) Maheu, F.S., Dozier, M., Guyer, A.E. *et al*, 'A preliminary study of medial temporal lobe function in youths with a history of caregiver deprivation and emotional neglect', *Cognitive, Affective & Behavioral Neuroscience*, 10 (1) 34–49, 2010.

(34) Tottenham, N., Hare, T.A., Millner, A. *et al*, 'Elevated amygdala response to faces following early deprivation, neurodevelopment and adversity', *Developmental Science*, 14 (2) 190–204, 2011.

(35) McCrory, E.J., De Brito, S.A., Sebastian, C.L. *et al*, 'Heightened neural reactivity to threat in child victims of family violence', *Current Biology*, 21 (23) R947–8, 2011.

(36) Jenness, J.L., Peverill, M., Miller, A.B. *et al*, 'Alterations in neural circuits underlying emotion regulation following child maltreatment: a mechanism underlying trauma-related psychopathology', *Psychol Med.*, 51 (11) 1880–9, 2021.

(37) McLaughlin, K.A., Sheridan, M.A., Gold, A.L. *et al*, 'Maltreatment exposure, brain structure, and fear conditioning in children and adolescents', *Neuropsychopharmacol*, 41 (8) 1956–64, 2016.

(38) Parker, S.W. and Nelson, C.A., 'The Bucharest Early Intervention Project Core Group: an event-related potential study of the impact of institutional rearing on face recognition', *Develop Psychopathol*, 17 (03), 2005.

(39) Moulson, M.C., Westerlund, A., Fox, N.A. *et al*, 'The effects of early experience on face recognition: an event-related potential study of institutionalized children in Romania', *Child Development*, 80 (4) 1039–56, 2009.

(40) Kungl, M.T., Bovenschen, I. and Spangler G., 'Early adverse caregiving experiences and preschoolers' current attachment affect brain responses during facial familiarity processing: an ERP study', *Front Psychol*, 8, 2047, 2017.

(41) Olsavsky, A.K., Telzer, E.H., Shapiro, M. *et al*, 'Indiscriminate amygdala response to mothers and strangers after early maternal deprivation', *Biological Psychiatry*, 74 (11) 853–60, 2013.

(42) Mesquita, A.R., Belsky, J., Crego, A. *et al*, 'Neural correlates of face familiarity in institutionally reared children with distinctive, atypical social behavior', *Child Development*, 86 (4) 1262–71, 2015.

(43) Makita, K., Takiguchi, S., Naruse, H. *et al*, 'White matter changes in children and adolescents with reactive attachment disorder: a diffusion tensor imaging study', *Psychiatry Research: Neuroimaging*, 303, 111129, 2020.

(44) Almas, A.N., Degnan, K.A., Radulescu, A. *et al*, 'Effects of early intervention and the moderating effects of brain activity on institutionalized children's social skills at age 8', *Proc Natl Acad Sci USA*, 109, 17228–31, 2012.

(45) Smith, K.E. and Pollak, S.D., 'Rethinking concepts and categories for understanding the neurodevelopmental effects of childhood adversity', *Perspect Psychol Sci.*, 16 (1) 67–93, 2021.

(46) Cassiers, L.L.M., Sabbe, B.G.C., Schmaal, L. *et al*, 'Structural and functional brain abnormalities associated with exposure to different childhood trauma subtypes: a systematic review of neuroimaging findings', *Front Psychiatry*, 9, 329, 2018.

CHAPTER 8

The Physical Health of Looked-After Children: A Neglected Topic?

Simon Ward

Introduction

Most children and young people who remain in care long-term have been abused and neglected, with compulsory measures used to separate them from their birth parents. It is understandable that there is considerable emphasis on the traumas that they have experienced, with accompanying emphasis on the insecurity of their attachments and other mental health challenges. By comparison, the state of their physical health is not so much debated.

However, an individual's physical health may inter-relate with his or her mental health; that is so for all individuals. Physical exercise, for example, may enhance an individual's sense of well-being while an inadequate diet may affect self-image, if seriously over or under weight. For looked-after children there may be additional associations with what they eat relating to availability and comfort.

Nevertheless, an aspiration for local authorities as corporate parents is to ensure that the health of children in care is at least as good as that of their overall peer group.

> Case example:
>
> Carl, aged 9, is in a specialist placement residential placement. His behaviour towards other children can

sometimes be unpredictable and aggressive. He has had various therapeutic interventions – cognitive-behavioural therapy, life-history, and so on. He has said that if neuro-linguistic therapy programming 'doesn't work, he 'doesn't know what he will do'.

He is interested in rugby – the walls of his room are plastered with information about St Helens Rugby League Club. At a placement review (and having consulted Carl), the social worker queried whether attending rugby training with the aim of attending matches – and the potential discipline, and friendships that could bring – might potentially be of as much benefit to him as organised therapies.

It is agreed that Carl would benefit from rugby training at a local club. With Carl's agreement, his key worker at the children's home is prepared to liaise with the club, explain something of Carl's position and take him to and collect him from training and matches. The managers at the home are uncertain whether they have resources to allow that.

The national context

In making such comparisons some acknowledgement should be made of dominant national discourses in relation to children's physical health. For example, their diet, weight and the amount of exercise that they take are inter-related factors that have received much publicity, with talk of problems in these areas that have reached 'pandemic' proportions (1). When considering health beliefs since the creation of the NHS, there has been a move from seeing medical professionals as those who will both solve and prevent ill health to greater emphasis upon individual responsibility. That perspective will influence the behaviour of local authorities having parental responsibility for children and young people in care, as well as the subjects themselves.

Concerns about standards of care for looked-after children

There are several reasons for assuming that children in care will be disadvantaged in relation to physical health. Generally, looked-after children come from economically poor backgrounds, with evidence that the recent growth in the number of children in care relates to increased poverty (2). There is a proven link between poor diet and income (3). In addition, parents' attention may have been diverted by mental illness, substance misuse, and the like, leaving limited encouragement within the home for sport and physical activities generally.

There have also been criticisms about the standards of parental care offered by local authorities. National statistics in relation to education, for instance, depict children and young people in care or who have recently left care as being very considerably behind in all aspects of educational attainment (4). Figures in relation to standards of physical health are not so readily available. However, local studies such as one in the London Borough of Tower Hamlets (5), as well as the whole of Scotland (6), would suggest that standards of dental health for this group are considerably below that of their peers, the latter study finding that extractions were twice as common. Debates continue as to the extent to which these disadvantages relate to backgrounds and experiences before or after children enter care – and the extent to which the present system 'fails' children (7, 8). A challenge for corporate care, with parental responsibilities being shared between birth parents and local authorities – foster and residential carers having delegated responsibilities – is who takes responsibility for health recommendations made at reviews. One study found that follow-up happened in only 54 per cent of cases (9). Parenting that is 'good enough' will sometimes depend on attention to detail, and also carers who have the confidence to discuss and question the views of professionals around them – not necessarily straightforward for those having day-to-day responsibilities for children in care.

The policy framework

The boarding-out regulations used by the post-war children's departments included expectations that health would be discussed when children in care had placement reviews and that they had regular medicals. It is only since local authorities adopted the looked-after children materials at the turn of the last century that guidelines for health assessments and planning for this group have been more detailed. In addition to health medicals (which teenagers who are Gillick-competent can refuse) each child in care has a health plan which should be considered at statutory reviews under the *Care Planning, Placement and Review Regulations, 2010*. Fostering Services Regulation 15 (2011) states that in addition to being registered with a GP a care provider must have:

> 'access to such medical, dental, nursing, psychological and psychiatric advice, treatment and other services as the child may require' and receive 'guidance, support

and advice on health, personal care and health promotion issues appropriate to the child's needs and wishes.'

At foster carer reviews 'Being Healthy' is one section that has to be completed in relation to the work that they are doing with a child they are fostering.

In addition, designated nurses and doctors must be identified in each area who will take a strategic interest in improving health outcomes for looked-after children, reflecting a need for multi-agency co-operation and input if efforts to improve the health of looked-after children are to be successful (10).

As with education plans, these developments appeared to represent clear improvements on what went before – if fully implemented. An impediment to improving the health of looked-after children can be changing placement while in care, as well as moving in and out of care. That may mean that continuity in terms of identifying individual health issues and treatments is lost, with a reluctance to register children with GPs if it is thought placements might be short term, appointment details being mislaid, and so on (10). Children may also suffer if parents don't share hereditary and other health-related details with subsequent carers, perhaps because they underestimate their importance or because they are reluctant to co-operate with key professionals.

Case example:

Lorna, 3, was placed for adoption soon after birth. She had suffered considerably with breathing problems, and following investigation was found to have cystic fibrositis, a genetic, hereditary condition. Nothing in the information about her medical background received before the adoption order was made had prepared her adoptive parents for this. Subsequent research with the help of the adoption support team has suggested that there is some history of cystic fibrositis within her birth father's family.

The physical health of looked-after children – possibilities for imaginative practice

Weight and diet

Obesity within the UK population and its relationship with diet, which has become now widely discussed by professionals, the public, and in the media, has particular ramifications for parenting. The quality of parenting experienced by looked-after children relies upon the resources and skills of foster and residential carers.

We know that children in care come disproportionately from low-income backgrounds and where family dynamics are also chaotic – factors likely to influence both the quality of food that they are offered before they come into care and, just as importantly, the circumstances in which eating takes place. There have been several local studies regarding obesity in looked-after children, however there does not seem to be consensus whether children in care are more likely to be overweight than their peers living with birth parents or, importantly, whether that group is likely to lose or gain weight while in care (12, 13, 14).

Detailed nutritional guidelines are available in relation to children of all ages in care and for care leavers (15). The importance of a balanced diet, not dominated by salt, sugars and processed foods, is highlighted in foster parent training, with some agencies providing Food in Care courses (16). It is also a matter considered and documented at foster carer reviews. Stirling University has produced a workshop facilitators' pack aiming to introduce participants to the symbolic implications of food (17). There are anecdotal examples illustrating the sometimes-complex relationship between emotions and food for children in care, which can make the requirement they have a healthy diet a challenging task.

Case example:

Kieran's mother was his main carer until he was four, but her life was dominated by drug taking, prostitution and poverty. His staple food at the time he came into care was curry, chips and a fizzy drink, although at 15kgs his weight gave no cause for concern. He has found it extremely difficult to adapt to the 'healthy diet' now offered to him, discarding green vegetables as 'yuk' and constantly asking for curry and chips. He eats these ravenously and has been found hiding bits of this meal under his bed. He eats mainly with his fingers. His foster carers are discussing with their supervising social worker how to combine listening to Kieran's preferences with the need to promote healthy eating. They see this as a gradual process: encouraging him to help putting food shopping lists together, explaining the origins of vegetables, having guessing games relating to the smell and texture of food, offering treats such as ice cream following a 'healthy' plate of food.

The balance aspect of diet is important: the local authority as corporate parent should be concerned about a healthy diet. There are further issues to consider for children in care in terms of children's rights to be involved in decisions about what they eat, and also emotions associated with eating and mealtimes. Mealtimes can be used as an opportunity to relax and communicate; on the other hand, children may react badly to over-strictness about food, refusing to eat for instance. They may have food preferences that evoke past memories, and the like. These are all factors that may be as important for children in care as dietary ones (18).

An important related matter is ensuring knowledge about dietary preferences of children whom carers are looking after is included in assessments when they enter care or change placement. A useful model here could be Essential Lifestyle Planning, an approach initially developed in relation to needs of people with learning disabilities (19). It recognises that new carers are often given insufficient information, and aims to improve quality of care, emphasizing individual need by detailing what is essential or important and preferences. That could apply to what food a child or young person wants to eat.

Purchasing and preparing food of good nutritional quality is a task that young people leaving care should be familiar with but which they themselves have identified frequently as being a skill which they lack (20). For this group, some of whom may have limited support from family, it should be part of the preparation process for leaving care.

On local levels there have been noteworthy attempts to improve awareness of nutritional issues amongst looked-after children and their carers. The Hearty Lives project in Liverpool was one example (21). Young people aged 11–17 and their carers (mainly foster parents and residential workers) were involved in a project to raise awareness of issues relating to diet and exercise, these included cooking and taste courses and workshops and food-growing workshops, as well as exercise sessions. A focus group of seven young people involved in the project from the local children in care council shared their ideas about keeping fit, exercise and healthy eating, exchanging ideas about healthy diet and related recipes.

A question about initiatives such as Hearty Lives is how lessons learnt can be integrated into everyday practices. Ultimately, the agency of carers, children and young people involved will be crucial in influencing and changing dominant discourses and cultures around 'being healthy'.

Exercise

As with diet, exercise can be a means of regulating weight, can contribute to general fitness, and is the subject of popular discussion about unhealthy sedentary lifestyles. Surveys by the Youth Sport Trust (22) indicated that the majority of parents were not aware of the NHS guidelines that 11 to 19-year-olds should have at least an hour of exercise every day, with only 45 per cent of young people averaging that amount during a week (23). The points already made in respect of diet and knowledge of child's preferences and capabilities will be relevant to exercise, as well as carers' knowledge and interest.

Some of the literature on looked-after children and exercise concentrates quite heavily on school sport (24), but it is important to remember that team sports may be anathema for some children and that there will be other contexts – in their lives with foster cars or in out of school clubs – in which fitness can be encouraged (25).

Case example:

At eight years of age Martin is facing a transfer from his present foster home to a 'permanent' one. Teachers say they find him to be a 'handful', particularly in terms of a tendency to get into scraps with other pupils; that he struggles to concentrate on school syllabus, including organised sport, although his proficiency at swimming and roller-blading has brought him some accolades from other children. His present foster carers recount how he initially found the countryside near them 'green and boring' but that turning walking into 'discovery' sessions sparked his enthusiasm. Martin's new foster father is a keen footballer and is looking forward to playing with him and introducing him in a local boys' team, wanting to encourage involvement in team sports.

Fitzgerald and colleagues (26) discussed an initiative in which young people in residential care were encouraged to increase physical training which helped them to lose weight. As with initiatives relating to diet and nutrition, a challenge is maintaining momentum in relation to such improvements and working out their relevance to all children and young people in care. There is an argument for exercising 'positive discrimination' in relation to this group, by making local authority sports centres free to looked-after children, as has happened in some areas (27).

Research elsewhere has involved young people more directly. In his participative study, involving five young men in residential care, Quarmby (28) identified three themes relating to their involvement in sport and exercise. The first was engagement with sport being disrupted by coming into care and changes of placement and/or school, with young people not always having the confidence or encouragement to continue. The second was institutional constraints, with young people requiring assistance – not always available – in getting to events where there was physical activity. Elsewhere, Quarmby and colleagues (29) give the example of 'Meg' not being allowed to have her picture taken with her football team, because of the need for corporate permission. The third theme related to 'sport as a means to an end', recognising the 'latent functions' that sport may have in making friends and contacts outside the care system, for example.

Promoting resilience is an important objective in relation to supporting children in care deal with the challenges of their lives (30). Developing skill in an area, such as football, can potentially raise confidence and a feeling of self-efficacy – that as an individual you can influence events though your own actions. This is helpful when tackling life challenges more generally. Such activities might also result in making a new group of friends, or involve interest or mentorship from others and help them to accumulate social capital, important resilience factors for children not living with their birth families (31).

Conclusion

Concerns about the quality of the citizen's physical health are common in professional and public discussion and not confined to children and young people in care. Because of poverty and parenting that has not been seen as 'good enough', assumptions can be made that looked-after children will be more disadvantaged than others of their age in health matters before they enter care – and that with the challenges of corporate parenting those disadvantages will continue. There is some evidence, research-based and anecdotal, for both those propositions although there are also examples of greater awareness and detailed associated assessments and interventions. Writing in 2000, Polnay and Ward (32) depicted health provisions for children in care that were inefficient and often ineffective – hopefully, increased interest and guidance means that practice has improved since then.

When reviewing the literature on physical well-being it is noticeable that, with some exceptions, the voices of children and young people in care are often muted or absent, relying heavily on those who were co-operative with researcher initiatives and on small samples. Greater understanding of their perspectives on this topic will no doubt be central to success in making improvements in this area. Initiatives in research, policy and awareness can all contribute positively in improving the well-being of looked-after children, but ultimately progress in this area will rely heavily on well-informed practice by carers, health workers and social workers and their ability to engage the young people they are involved with (33).

References

(1) Editorial, 'Childhood obesity: a growing pandemic', *The Lancet Diabetes & Endocrinology*, January 2022.

(2) Bennett, D., Mason K., Schlüter, D. *et al*, 'Trends in inequalities in children looked after in England between 2004 and 2019: a local area ecological analysis', *BMJ Open* 10, 2020.

(3) Food Foundation, *Broken Plate Report*, London: 2021.

(4) Department for Education, *National Statistics: Children looked after in England, including adoption: 2020 to 2021*, 2021.

(5) Local Government Association, *Healthy Futures: Supporting and promoting the health needs of looked-after children*, 2016.

(6) McMahon, A., Elliot, L., Macpherson, L. *et al*, 'Inequalities in the dental health needs and access to dental services among looked-after children in Scotland', *Archives of Disease in Childhood*, 103, 39–43, 2018.

(7) Little, M., 'Looked-after children: can services ever succeed?', *Adoption and Fostering* 34 (2) 3–7, 2010.

(8) Sinclair, I., 'Looked-after children: can services ever succeed? A different view', 8–13, *Adoption and Fostering*, 34 (2) 2010.

(9) Croft, G. 'Implementation of health recommendations after initial statutory health assessment', *Adoption and Fostering*, 33 (2) 76–81, 2009.

(10) Department for Education, *Promoting the Health and Well-being of Looked-after Children*, 2015.

(11) Croft, as above, (9).

(12) Hadfield, S. and Preece, P., 'Obesity in looked-after children: is foster care protective from the dangers of obesity?', *Child: care, health and development*, 34 (6) 710–712, 2008.

(13) Croft, G. and Frith, K., 'Obesity in looked-after children: findings of a local audit and strategies for intervention', *Adoption and Fostering*, 35 (2) 86–90, 2011.

(14) Bailey, E., Teh, C., Peet, H., 'Audit of looked-after children (LAC) in residential care and BMI increase in one UK local authority', *Adoption and Fostering*, 45 (3) 339–347, 2021.

(15) Carolyn Walker Trust, *Eating Well for Looked-after Children: Nutritional and Practical Guidelines – Report of an Expert Working Group*, London: Carol Walker Trust, 2001.

(16) National Fostering Group, *Food in Care*, Uxbridge: NFG, 2022.

(17) Emond, R., George, C., McIntosh, I. and Punch, S., *Food for Thought: Facilitators' Pack*, University of Stirling, 2013.

(18) Emond, R., McIntosh, I., Punch, S. and Lightowler, C., *Children, Food and Care (Insight 22)*. Institute for Research and Innovation in Social Services: Glasgow: IRISS, 2013.

(19) Smull, M. and Sanderson, H., *Essential Lifestyle Planning for Everyone*, London: Helen Sanderson Associates, 2005.

(20) Emond, R. *et al*, as above, (18).

(21) Medforth, N., Evans, J., Hills, M. *et al*, 'Hearty Lives (Liverpool): a case study-based evaluation of a project designed to promote healthy eating and lifestyles in looked after young people', *Adoption and Fostering*, 43 (1) 75–88, 2019.

(22) Youth Sport Trust, Yougov survey, 2019.

(23) Sport England, *Active Lives, Children and Young People Survey, London: Sport England*, p. 5, 2021.

(24) Sandford, R., Quarmby, T., Hooper, O. and Duncombe, R., 'Exercising their right to be active? Care-experienced young people's perspectives on physical education and school sport', *Physical Education Matters*, Summer 2020.

(25) O'Donnell, C., Sandford, R. and Parker, A., 'Physical education, school sport and looked-after children', *Sport, Education and Society*, 25 (6) 605–617, 2019.

(26) Fitzgerald, N., Aherne, C., Gaynor, D. *et al*, 'Developing mental and physical wellness for looked-after young people through a fitness and nutritional guidance programme', *Scottish Journal of Residential Childcare*, 13 (2) 2014.

(27) Macfarlane, H., 'A sporting chance for looked-after children', *Third Force News*, 7th February 2017.

(28) Quarmby, T. 'Sport and physical activity in the lives of looked-after children: a 'hidden group' in research, policy and practice', *Sport, Education and Society*, 19 (7) 944–958, 2014.

(29) Quarmby, T., Sandford, R., Hooper, H. and Duncombe, R., 'Narratives and marginalised voices: storying the sport and physical activity experiences of care-experienced young people', *Qualitative Research in Sport, Exercise and Health*, 13 (3) 426–437, 2021.

(30) Gilligan, R., *Promoting Resilience: A resource guide on working with children in the care system*, London, BAAF, 2009.

(31) Quarmby, T. *et al*, as above, (29).

(32) Polnay, L. and Ward, H., 'Promoting the health of looked-after children', *British Medical Journal*, 320, 661–662, 2000.

(33) The author would like to thank Hayley Grier, an MA student at Liverpool John Moores University, for sharing her endeavours to encourage children she fosters to adopt a healthy lifestyle.

CHAPTER 9

How Life Stories Can Heal Traumatised Children and Families

Richard Rose

Introduction

Many years ago, I was fortunate to co-write a book with Terry Philpot all about therapeutic life story work. It was called *The Child's Own Story* (1) and it introduced a model of practice that is now used worldwide. When the publishers sent the manuscript to be read by assessors, the response from a leading charity was: 'Why would the author want to bring the past back into the present, children should be allowed to move on, to forget and start their lives anew'.

If only the brain, the body and the individual's spirit were that simple to control, to, in effect, erase the past, not be the formation of it; to be capable of forgetting the hurt and the pain, not to grow and live with it. If we could have a switch that could just say goodbye to the trauma of our past, of the challenges of our family, our self, and to just live for today, would I, would you, would anyone use it?

Not so long ago my father passed away; his death was very sad, but we had notice of his impending end. When he died, I recalled much of the story we developed together, and the experience of grief and loss followed on from this. I haven't stopped grieving my father, but I have learned to live with the grief, for it to be accepted as a present but not to become a driver of my future. There will be times as you live with grief and loss that the memories and the emotions of the hurt can be ever present, and for some these will be repetitive memories where the impact of certain past trauma hurts as much, or sometimes more, than the original event.

This chapter considers the importance of understanding the past, and by doing so, to make sense of the present and, consequently, be freed to shape the future.

There are many definitions of trauma; however, I do not believe that trauma is the event itself, it is the residual left after the event. All of us could experience the same traumatic event, but not one of us would react in the same way. Not one of us will have the same emotional, physical, cognitive, spiritual, or sensory reaction, as we are all unique, and so our traumas and our stories are also unique. The important word within some trauma definitions is 'residual' – what remains, the unresolved hurt. I explain it as our ghosts of the past. Why the concept of ghosts?

(i) Get a sheet of paper, draw a ghost on the far left of the piece of paper; next, consider three words that might describe your ghost, words like 'memories', 'insubstantial', 'corner of the eye movement', 'frightening', or 'unwelcome'. Next, think of a moment in your life that sometimes resurfaces to your present – it could be a good memory or difficult one. Where does this memory come from? How is it still there? More importantly, what are you feeling at this moment and how are you coping with this? What is happening in your heart and your body? At the end of this exercise, think what it must be like if you were not consciously seeking this memory, but the memory is constantly seeking you? Ghosts are real.

Alongside trauma, we have the manifestation of its impact.

(ii) Get another piece of paper and on the far-left side draw a monster. Once you have drawn your picture, think of three words that might describe this monster. These could include 'angry', 'dangerous', overwhelming' and maybe 'safe', or 'protective'. Now ask yourself a question: 'Do I have a monster in me?', and put 'Yes' or 'No' next to the description.

If you do not have a monster in you, I would be worried about you! It might be when you get cross and shout at someone; or you swear and instantly realise that was not appropriate. It could be due to road rage or through running away or towards the stimuli of the moment, you might understand it as a reaction to your loss of internal control; where you are now vulnerable and scared, so you respond to this by subconsciously responding for survival.

Our monster serves a purpose, in the main to protect us when we lose our internal control, when we are vulnerable and fearful (although we might not understand this at the time). If it helps, think of it as your safety valve, your personal failsafe! This can be a default, a go-to at times of stress, but its purpose is to push the threat away, to gain space to reclaim control and assess the risk. Does this work for you?

> (iii) On the paper next to 'Yes', describe your monster when it responds, and then think of the outcome of your monster's appearance.

It certainly works for me; despite my emotions afterward, I can understand that when all else fails, I must protect my 'self'.

> (iv) When your monster has done what it needed to and resided back in your space, think about how would you feel then? You might feel shameful, embarrassed, relieved, exhausted. Finally, place these emotional aftermaths next to the monster traits.

In both the ghosts and the monster papers you now have a sequence of response to overwhelming events – both ghosts and monsters are real.

Nearly 25 years ago, Stansbury and colleagues (2) found that children who live in chaotic environments learn techniques to keep them safe. These techniques are coping strategies that are in the main 'defence-based'. If the chaos they experience continues and becomes a constant, these strategies become behaviour. For many traumatised children, carrying the hurt of the past enables them to see threat quickly and, in the fear that results, revert to their default behaviour to protect their self. For highly traumatised children who have had monstrous things happen to them, their survival behaviours can seem monstrous. It is hard sometimes to remember that what the child is doing is for safety and survival, but it is all driven by the past and based on the 'what works' principle.

In my work with traumatised children and young people that have as part of their defence systems, aggression, and challenging behaviour,

I need to help them see that 'how they defended' and 'how they survived' has been shaped through the trauma exposure that have occurred and, in some cases, still impact on them.

> Case example:
>
> I worked with an 11-year-old who told me she would be in fear of going to school and coming back to her foster carers. It was not the school or the home that was the difficulty, it was the journey, which she would make on foot. Her fear was that her birth father might be looking for her and he might try and take her away, that her birth father would be waiting after school and try and hurt her again. This young girl had already experienced four years in care and she had not seen her birth family since; she was in a secure and loving placement, but her residual fears were dominant in those moments and, as such, are most vulnerable. On one of the sessions with me, she explained that she saw her father in a car by the school and she had 'run for her life'.
>
> The sad thing in this case was that no one had told her that her father had died two years previously. It was not an oversight, but a purposeful decision by the social services department. I was asked to carry out therapeutic life story work and so it was decided that I would tell her about this. When I told her about her father's death, she became upset and then thoughtful about him. We went to his grave and on the way back she said: 'I can go to school safe now, my fear won't be there anymore as he cannot hurt me'. This residue was resolved and over a short period of time, her school engagement and her education performance improved as her preoccupation lowered.

As Stephen King reminds us: '[the] truth is that monsters are real, and ghosts are real, too. They live inside us, and sometimes they win' (3).

How do we reach our very, very challenging children and young people? How do we make sense of why they do the things they do? Quite simply, it is to provide them with a systemic approach that encourages their carer and the therapeutic life story worker to bear witness to their journey and their stories, and, in doing so, we help them to understand the ghosts of the past and, together, help them to tame the monsters of their present.

As we grow, we learn how to keep ourselves safe. If we are fortunate to have parental figures to do this for us when we need them the most, we learn that when we can't keep our selves safe; our carers can, and do. Children who have learnt that adults cannot keep them safe, learn to do this to the best of their own ability. These children create ways in which they can manage the world, but this might look and/or feel very distressing, combative, or challenging in its operation. At the heart of this distressing behaviour, is the need every one of us have – the need to be safe.

Traumatised children (and adults) often exist in crises and try to survive each day rather than planning for their tomorrow. They often live in fear, but then they manage that fear by developing responses that may increase risks to decrease fear, to give meaning to the emotional turmoil within. When their internal world is so frightening and the external world is dull, to equate their internal drive they may engage in behaviour that replicates or diverts from their state of self. We will see children self-harm, take drugs, become very aggressive and violent, exhibit sexualised behaviours, or become vulnerable to those that exploit them – all of which culminates in immeasurable harm but also confirms their lack of esteem, their worthlessness, and the inability to be lovable.

What we try and do is help children understand that you do not have to be led by your past, that your past can't be rewritten. It has happened. Once you can make sense of your past and the way it may control you is when you are freer to make decisions to live your present and shape your future.

Case example:

Tom (not his real name) was a 9-year-old boy with whom I worked several years ago. He had been placed in 21 different care settings and was, at the time, awaiting his 22nd placement. He understood that adults can't keep him safe, so he had to keep himself safe. When adults tried and showed him love he saw that as dangerous, so he had to push that away. He told me that he had been 'therapised to death'. This is not a negative comment on therapy, but a reality that he had been subject to many therapy interventions, but none had the desired impact.

When I was asked to work with him, I said to him: 'I'm Richard, nice to see you'. He looked at me and he said: 'Well, my name is Tom and I have a monster in me, and I like him'.

> If I had replied by asking: 'Well, what's the monster's name? What do you like about your monster? It must be hard for you; or do you find it hard; or how does this monster protect you?', I would have potentially reminded him of a therapy process that many people have used but all had failed him. He needed to do something different, an approach that might not be questions but reflections from the adult perspective.
>
> I responded to his statement by simply telling him the truth: 'That's really interesting because I've got a monster in me, too'. He looked at me and then he said: 'Well, what's your monster like? What does your monster do? Does your monster get you in trouble like my monster' – and suddenly, I had a very different relationship, a connection where he was setting the pace, the topic, and the opportunity.

Ghosts and monsters can 'pop in' the back of our heads, and some of us can manage that and others can't. Every single child and young person I've worked with has had monsters and ghosts that exist in the world around them and within. That isn't helpful for them because they use behaviours which, when presented are countered by the carer in a defensive or critical way.

I have never worked with a monster, but I work with children and adults who have had the most monstrous things happen to them. Understanding the past of the children that we are working with can support our approach and avoid counter transference of unwelcome, or confused transference from the hurt child. Unless we help to unravel the past, how can we progress the child to a safer future?

If I can help children understand that some of these threats and experiences that they were shaped by in their early years are no longer valid for them, that these experiences of enduring and/or witnessing abuse can be thought through, can be understood to be a part of history but not the drivers of the present and future, then we can have recovery. As children understand that their current protective behaviours are no longer needed, we can encourage their immediate carers and those influencing them to forge new behaviours and healthier strategies for their future.

What we need to understand is that children have a history and if we understand the history, we can understand then how they make sense of their world. We need to be consistent, predictable, repetitive in all the things that we do. By doing so, the child doesn't have to wonder what, but know. The better the relationships we can forge *with* the child, and as importantly, those *around* the child, the more that we can have congruence, and the more likely that child is going to say, 'Well, maybe you are different'; and carers might see and understand that behaviours that are intolerable, undesirable, sometimes unmanageable come from experiences that have shaped the child they care for. If we can support all those around the child, if we can work with our child to make sense of the past, then maybe we can move forward with the child, and support them to move forward themselves.

I would expect that you, as you are reading this chapter, are thinking of other things such as home, health, your job, and your family. When you are engaged in an activity, you may find that there are other demands for your attention, or that a thought won't stop its presentation and so will drag you from listening or paying attention to the current situation. This is often referred to as preoccupation. If your preoccupation is very demanding, you might start to misread, to skip or to give up reading this chapter altogether.

Case example:

A 12-year-old, with whom I worked, had a history of child sexual exploitation. I tried to engage her in thinking about her past, but each time I tried she would react by small behavioural traits that said: 'I can't talk about this, it is too dangerous and too scary', but presented as shouting, hitting and anger. On the fourth session she said to me: 'I know why I need to work with you, Richard.' I said, 'What's happened?' and she replied: 'We were doing bar charts in school and while I was in school doing bar charts, I was thinking about lots of different things, and I managed to work out that there was too much in my brain'.

I asked if she could help me understand what she had worked out.

She asked me to draw a bar chart on the paper we use to talk about her life (I use rolls of wallpaper, so that we can develop a pictorial tapestry of the child's journey). I did as she asked. Once done, she asked me to write in the bar chart what she had been thinking about. She said: 'I was thinking about my mum.' So I had to write the following down in the bar chart. She said: 'My mum had alcohol issues. She'd get drunk, she'd fall, often she'd be sick.'

She then said that she would make sure mum was OK. She'd look after her two younger siblings and then at night-time she'd keep coming downstairs to make sure that mum was still OK. Her role in the family was to make sure that mum was OK. and to parent the little children. Once done, I asked about this memory, which was three years old, as she had been in the care of the local authority for some time. I asked if there was a reason for thinking about this in class and she told me that this was a regular thought and that she was waiting for the police to come to tell her that her mum was dead. That nobody was there to look after her and that it would be her fault if this did happen as she should be there to care for her mother.

She then asked me to make the bar chart taller. I did so and then she told me that she was also thinking about her brother, Ben. Her brother had been adopted three years previously and the adoptive family promised that they would write to her every six months so she would know that Ben was OK. They have never written to her. She held this boy in her head because she cannot afford to let her brother disappear. She then added her fears about her birth father. He was in prison for assaulting her mother and her mother's brother. Her social worker had told her that her dad was being released. The little girl was afraid he would go home and assault mum again, and she wouldn't be there to protect her. She reached over me and her carer, and she closed the bar chart but left a little space at the top. She said: 'With all this in my head, I only had this much left to learn maths.'

To really understand this, draw a bar chart and write from the bottom upwards what is preoccupying you, and each area will take away your space to be present for reading or continuing to read this.

Imagine a school class, most of the children are alert and ready to learn. Many children have little to worry them and have the capacity to be present, and over the next hour or so, they process all that is there to learn. In the class though, there may well be a child who has much in his or her head – hunger, worries, memories, ghosts of the past, fear of the present; each takes up space in the brain and is, therefore, full of preoccupation. The teaching starts and before long the child may become overwhelmed: they have no space for this learning and so stop learning as the information is overflowing. The child can't hear any more, they are overwhelmed, but they may see that other children seem to be managing. Fear evolves as the child starts to realise that they are not able to stay on task – and what if the teacher were to ask questions? The other children might see that they are not as clever as they are, so what can the child do to feel safe? The simple response is to make space. She may need her monster to create chaos in order to survive: this child may start to nudge another child, start to throw things at another child, or start to make noises in the class. He or she may need to disrupt the class so that they're not exposed as being weak, stupid, not good enough or similar shame. If that works the first, second, and the third time why on earth wouldn't they do the same thing when the same threat occurs?

Think about a foster child, after a hard day at school. He or she gets home and the carer says something like: 'Go to your bedroom, take your school clothes off; put the dirty clothes in the laundry basket; have a wash; put your play stuff on; and then come down to the kitchen'. This child might get to their bedroom and will not know what to do next – what's happened? They haven't done anything because they haven't managed to hear anything other than the initial instructions. They are now upstairs thinking: 'What am I supposed to be doing?' The carer gets angry because the child has not done what they have been told to do; the child is already anticipating the anger and may need to create another event so that the carer will forget what they told them to do in the first place.

> A 9-year-old child said to me:
>
> 'When you are at school or at home and you don't know if you are safe, you have to try people out, to see if they can keep me safe. If they can, I am safe. If they can't, well, then, I have to keep myself safe. I become an angry lion, an angry animal, or person so that I can scare people away.'

Think of it a different way. You're in the roller coaster car with all your favourite people in it. You've got this massive climb to the top of the ride, then a steep drop, followed by the loop, the loops projecting you to the end. As you sit in the car, and before the ride starts, a fairground worker comes over and places the safety bar against your lap and the laps of those sharing the car with you. What do you do next? I would check the bar is in place. I would give it a real shake and expect it to stay in place. If it does, I feel safe and I can enjoy the ride. What if, on trying the bar, it moved up? It would mean I am no longer safe – how would you react? I know I would have to get myself safe. This is no different to our hurt children in care: the roller coaster is their placement and role of the carers is like the bar on the car which keeps us safe.

Every so often I might not feel safe in my placement, I may have noticed problems in the home, arguments, or worries – can my carer still keep me safe? I may try out the bar (my carer), I might revert to previous behaviour to see if my bar (my carer) can keep me safe. If they respond by saying, 'Hey, it's OK, there are a few worries but nothing that will stop me keeping you safe', then I might feel safe in the chaos around me. If, rather than reacting positively, the carer replies by saying, 'Don't you start, can't you see I am struggling? Get out of my way, I can't cope with you as well right now'.

Then, there is only me to keep me safe and so I go back to the behaviours that have served me well.

With all the cases presented above, and the thoughts about monsters and ghosts that live inside us, I hope that this chapter helps to explain the essential role that stories and narrative intervention play in supporting children's trauma recovery. In telling their story, we can bear witness and hold the child's pain whilst we share other stories of those involved in their journey. This provides the time and space to assist in reframing the narrative as a more informed and therapeutic story that has dealt with shame, guilt, confusion, anger, and the unknown.

All of us are a collection of stories that represent what we were to who we are. In understanding our story, we can move forward to a future not constrained or defined by the unresolved past. Stories are meaning, stories help us make sense, stories are something to lean on (4).

References

(1) Rose, R. and Phipot, T., *The Child's Own Story. Life Story Work with Traumatised Children*. London: Jessica Kingsley Publishers, 2004.

(2) Stansbury, K and Harris, M L., 'Individual differences in stress reactions during peer entry episode', *Journal of Experimental Child Psychology*, 76, 50–63, 2000.

(3) King, S., *The Shining*, London: Hodder Headline, 1977.

(4) Rose, R., *Closing keynote address to the 2nd International Conference on Therapeutic Life Story Work*, Melbourne Australia, 2022.

CHAPTER 10

Poverty and Children in Care: The Challenges for Social Work

Richard Machin, Fungisai Mushawa and Jennifer Simpson

Introduction

This chapter explores the links between poverty and children coming into care. Attention is given to the connection between policy and socio-economic disadvantage. It also examines the ways in which poverty increases childhood vulnerability and how practitioners respond to this. We argue for a greater professional appreciation of structural factors which underpin poverty, and identify a need for a change in practice to work more effectively with service users who are challenged by the daily adversities of living in poverty.

A look at the figures

In 1999 the UK government committed to a 20-year target to end child poverty (1). However, official poverty figures for 2019–20 show that over three million children live in poverty, a reduction of just 200,000 compared to 1998–99 (2). Even more worryingly, child poverty rates are increasing, and all reliable projections predict that this will continue (3). UK poverty rates have attracted international attention. In 2018 the United Nations Special Rapporteur on extreme poverty and human rights, Professor Philip Alston, visited the UK and concluded:

> 'For almost one in every two children to be poor in twenty-first century Britain is not just a disgrace, but a social calamity and an economic disaster, all rolled into one.' (4)

The fluctuating trends in child poverty over the last 20 years clearly demonstrate the influence of policy. Child Poverty Action Group (5) identified three distinct phases in child poverty during this period: steady progress from 1999–2005, rises before progress resumed from 2005–2010, and sustained rises from 2010 to the present. The figures referred to below represent the number of children in low-income households before housing costs (the government define this as having below 60 per cent of the median household income (6). In the first period, there was a consistent reduction in child poverty rates from 3.4 million to 2.7 million. The Labour government introduced a range of policies considered influential in reducing child poverty rates. The National Minimum Wage was introduced in 1999 (7), and Working Tax Credit and Child Tax Credit in 2003. Despite well-publicised administrative problems, tax credits provided targeted support for families and significantly reduced child poverty rates (8). There were significant investments in education and early years provision, although critics state that more fundamental improvements were impeded by a commitment to market choice and competition (9).

A more complex picture emerges in the period 2005–2010: child poverty rates increased to 2.9 million by 2007–2008, followed by two years of decline. Policy tensions are evident here with increased investment in welfare benefits but a move away from the idea of 'welfare rights' to a 'creeping conditionality' (10): benefits and services are increasingly dependent on an individual's behaviour and obligations (11). The global financial crisis resulted in the loss of over a million UK jobs; the fall in the GDP was the most significant since the Great Depression (12).

Figures and finance

Child poverty figures from 2010 onwards make for depressing reading. The number of children in low-income households has risen from 2.3 million in 2010–11 to 3.2 million in 2019–20. The pace of this negative trajectory is stark: it took 12 years for child poverty to fall by a million, but only six years for this to be reversed, over three million children live in poverty for the first time in nearly 20 years, and rates are increasing at a rate not seen since the 1980s (13). UK austerity policies have had a disproportionate impact on those on the lowest incomes; while links have been established between austerity measures and suicide, food insecurity, mental health, and homelessness.

During this period the social security budget has been cut by over £30 billion. This sustained programme of welfare reform has resulted in a startling increase in child vulnerability. The combined impact of the roll-out of Universal Credit, the two-child limit for benefits (14), and the benefit cap has resulted in a significant increase in the numbers of low-income families who are struggling to manage everyday expenses. The cumulative impact of welfare reform has left families who rely on welfare benefits, on average, nearly £3,500 per year worse off (15).

The findings of the Social Metrics Commission

A new multi-dimensional measurement of poverty has been developed by the Social Metrics Commission. (The SMC is a non-partisan organisation (16) which considers not only material resources, but also the availability of liquid assets, disability, childcare, and housing costs.) The latest SMC data collected before the onset of COVID-19, in the period April 2018 to March 2019, found that 4.5 million, or 33 per cent, of all children live in poverty (17).

A complex picture is revealed: lone parents are much more likely to live in poverty than full-time working couples with children. Poverty rates remain highest among families with children and are significantly higher for black and minority ethnic households. A poverty rate of 46 per cent was recorded for families where the head of the household is black, African, Caribbean, or black British, compared to a rate of 19 per cent where the household head is white. There are strong links between disability and poverty, with 50 per cent of all those experiencing poverty living in a family with a disabled person.

The SMC has developed a series of Lived Experience Indicators which establish links between poverty and vulnerability. These demonstrate that 20 per cent of people experiencing poverty live in families with no formal qualifications, 27 per cent are behind with paying bills, and 70 per cent have no savings. The SMC data reveals the entrenched nature of poverty, with 7.1 million people experiencing poverty in two of the last three years, and 4.5 million living in the deepest poverty, measured as being more than 50 per cent below the poverty line (18).

The impact of poverty on vulnerable children

The Institute of Health Equity has highlighted the regressive impact of a decade of austerity, with particularly negative outcomes for lone parent families, people with disabilities and from minority ethnic families:

> 'Family circumstances, so vital for development in the early years and for young people, have deteriorated for many since 2010.' (19)

With poverty comes the increased risk of adverse childhood experiences such as abuse and neglect, mental health problems, drug, or alcohol misuse, and living in care. The impact of deprivation on childhood vulnerability cannot be overstated, and the last decade has been a particularly troubling one.

A child's vulnerability means exposure to more risks than other children of their age and having one or more risk factors in their lives. Poverty makes children vulnerable to living in conditions of deprivation. The World Bank's downward spiral of childhood vulnerability demonstrates that with each risk factor, the child's vulnerability increases, exposing the child to new risks. Risk factors can result from any change that affects the child's development (20); extreme poverty is a major determinant of vulnerability for children. In 2020, Bennett et al highlighted that child poverty is a contributory factor in child abuse and neglect (21) while in 2016 Bywaters et al stated (22):

> 'Growing up in adverse socio-economic circumstances is an important risk factor for child abuse and neglect and for children being taken into care, with poverty, unemployment and parental financial stress recognised as contributory causal factors.'

The impact of Covid-19

The Covid-19 crisis will have a lasting impact on children living on low incomes. The closure of schools and reduction in support networks, which are protective factors for children, has led to increased vulnerability for many children which may go unnoticed by professionals (23). Schweiger suggests a vulnerable child is more likely to be harmed and require protection (24). Beddoe and Keddell highlighted the stigma and shame that can be associated with poverty and the need for social workers to intervene in ways that do not reinforce this poverty stigma (25). They suggested intervention with an emotional response and one that does not obscure the structural and economic causes of problems (26).

The impact of social disadvantage

Research on inequality in UK child welfare interventions suggests that social work practice is concerned with risk management and interventionist approaches that can be mapped directly across to levels of poverty and disadvantage (27). The Assessment Framework is a tool used by social workers to assess how the different aspects of a child's life impacts on their development, highlighting areas that are crucial in meeting a child's developmental needs such as parenting capacity and family environmental factors (28). Gupta emphasised that practitioners can overlook and fail to assess adequately socio-economic factors, with poverty often slipping out of sight in assessments (29). Poverty has an impact on parenting and can lead to an inability to meet the child's needs, which is likely to result in a failure to protect or support the child. This can be amplified by a lack of resources in the community (for example, children's centres), and an absence of wider family networks. Changes in the environment in which children are growing can adversely influence their development and the impact of the Covid-19 pandemic, welfare reform, rising costs and low wages have exacerbated existing vulnerabilities for families, increasing the likelihood of children ending up in care. Burgess et al suggested that assessments of neglect should focus explicitly on the impact of wider social and environmental factors that place pressure on parents and affect children's lives; packages of intervention need to address these factors. Research by Bywaters highlighted that 'neighbourhood deprivation significantly affects a child's chances of being subject to a child protection intervention' (30).

A media report quoted 12 directors of children services in the North East of England, who acknowledged children go into care as a consequence of poverty (31). They suggested national measures to reduce poverty, focused on raising family incomes, are needed to break the cycle of deprivation which is driving concerns about child welfare. Social workers can only respond effectively if such measures are in place to support their role.

Where do we go from here? Models and guidance

With growing numbers of children going into care (32), the government needs to support local authorities in areas of deprivation as an inability to do so increases the vulnerability for children. In 2021, the number of children looked-after by local authorities in England increased to its highest ever level of over 80,000. The responsibility for safeguarding children should not be left to social workers.

With increasing poverty levels, social workers need additional resources to support children and prevent children entering care. There is a conflict between the expectation that social workers will accelerate care proceedings and wider structural issues, such as poverty, which cannot be overcome within a set period of time. This adds to the risk factors for children in poorer families becoming susceptible to care. A study by Morris revealed that poverty has become invisible in practice (33).

Preventing and tackling poverty should be part of the everyday role for social workers, if equipped with adequate tools.

This chapter has made reference to the continuing criticism of the way in which practitioners seem to be blind to the deleterious effects of poverty on service users. The preoccupation of practitioners with eliminating risk and their prevailing attitudes about poverty pathologises service users. This fails to appreciate the physical and psychological effects poverty has on the ability to parent (34, 35, 36, 37). Added to this is what O'Brien describes as the focus of practitioners on individualism and individualisation (34). This means that there is an expectation that change will come via parents, without any consideration of wider structural issues. It is apparent that the integral element of the social work role that is concerned with social justice has in effect been lost to high caseloads (35) along with an organisational approach that is influenced by neo-liberalism (36); government policy that is predisposed to 'rescuing' children (37); and practitioner responses that are impelled by a sense of moral duty towards children but, fails to appreciate that the rights of parents and children are not in opposition, but are interwoven (38).

Attempts have been made to respond to the criticisms outlined above in a range of practice guidance documents and suggested practice models that include the British Association of Social Work (39); and the Anti-Poverty Practice Framework for Social Work in Northern Ireland (40); Relational Poverty Analysis (41); Poverty Aware Practice (PAP)(42); and the extension of this by Saar-Heiman and Gupta which has led to the development of the Poverty Aware Paradigm for Child Protection (43).

Common to all the practice guidance and models is the need for practitioners to work alongside service users living in poverty, appreciating that they are experts in their lived experience. Practitioners should be prepared to learn from service users about their coping strategies for living with poverty (44). This clearly indicates the importance of relationship-based practice, where the emphasis is upon making sense of, and seeking to, address the emotional impact and past traumatic events on individuals. The advantage of this approach is that it exposes practitioners to the effects of poverty and allows them opportunity to engage in strength-based approaches that recognise wider contextual issues such as material deprivation, shame, and oppression (45).

In terms of completing assessments and other reports, Krumer-Nevo (46) states the language used should be specific and describe the daily challenges faced allowing for subsequent interventions that are not only co-produced in conjunction with the service user, but also speak to material deprivation.

Another area highlighted is the need for practitioners to appreciate that awareness within practice 'belongs across the whole social work continuum from prevention to care and control' (47). This means practitioners should take account of the socio-economic circumstances of service users and consider how, and to what extent, the risks identified are rooted in the individualised behaviours of service users or are a reaction to financial exploitation. The models and guidance documents also recognise the importance of income maximisation (48) and the need for practitioners to make this an integral part of their interventions.

Linked to the above is advocacy. It is recognised as not only speaking on behalf of service users but also advocating for resources, challenging micro-aggressions, and making prominent that poverty is a violation of human rights, as well as encouraging service users to make their voices heard (49). Lastly, common to the guidance documents and the PAP model is the call for practitioners to support and promote community empowerment (50) while recognising the community as both the harbinger of, and solution to, poverty.

There is clear evidence to suggest that social care organisations have a significant role to play in ameliorating the effects of poverty through 'poverty proofing' activities such as changing policies and procedures, building partnerships and alliances, as well as critically reviewing the practice models used by social work practitioners (51). This requires, in the first instance, the gathering of data regarding the socio-economic circumstances of those served by social care organisations and making use of these details to inform services. Additionally, service users should influence the development of policy and practice (52). Both the practice guidance documents, and PACP highlight the role of senior leaders, recognising that they are in a position to consider the strategic allocation of resources (53). The BASW practice guidance (54) encourages the development and building of partnerships and inter-agency alliances with other third sector bodies such as local food banks, religious organisations, and specific community groups. By doing so, social care organisations are able to expand their network of influence and create strategic interventions specifically designed to counter draconian and oppressive policy measures (55).

Furthermore, where a local authority makes use of a specific practice model, they too are open to scrutiny via a policy aware lens. Dewanckel (56) has commented that Signs of Safety (a strengths-based approach to child safeguarding work) falls short in terms of considering wider structural issues such as poverty, and the same is true for systemic practice where the emphasis is upon developing trusting relationships that motivate change. With its approach being built upon psycho-social and therapeutic interventions there is little attention given to poverty. It is suggested that organisations adapt the practice models to remove 'poverty blindness' and raise awareness among practitioners.

Of the poverty aware models and guidance reviewed, only the Northern Ireland Department of Health (57) makes mention of education. Yet before a practitioner embarks on a social work career, they are subject to training from higher education institutions. This highlights that there is an active and much-needed role for social work educators to play. Krumer-Nevo *et al* (58) consider why poverty has not featured more prominently in the curriculum of social work education programmes. They refer to poverty being considered 'natural' or 'normal' among marginalised groups that practitioners regularly work with. Crucially, in so doing, they infer that social work educators are also poverty blind.

As a way forward it is suggested that the causes and consequences of poverty should be key components in the curriculum of social work education, and that students should be provided with a practice framework. Furthermore, postgraduate training should raise awareness. Such training should sit alongside mental health, child abuse and neglect, as well as adverse childhood experiences (59).

Conclusion

As we have shown, poverty levels have risen alarmingly over the past 10 years and this has increased the vulnerabilities of children. These vulnerabilities have not gone unnoticed by practitioners, but their responses have not always been grounded and informed by an awareness of poverty. As has been stated, this means that:

> 'If the underlying causes for their poverty are not well understood it appears that the responses to child poverty are also merely treating symptoms. Or, to put it differently, the causes of child poverty should be eradicated, but for that structural changes are needed' (60).

References

(1) Blair, Tony, Beveridge Lecture, 18 March 1999.
https://www.bristol.ac.uk/poverty/downloads/background/Tony%20Blair%20Child%20Poverty%20Speech.doc

(2) Office for National Statistics, *Households Below Average Income for Financial Years ending 1995 to 2020.* London: Department for Work and Pensions, 2021. https://www.gov.uk/government/statistics/households-below-average-income-for-financial-years-ending-1995-to-2020

(3) Hood, A. and Waters, T., *Living Standards, Poverty and Inequality in the UK: 2017–18 to 2021–22.* London: Institute for Fiscal Studies, 2017. https://ifs.org.uk/uploads/publications/comms/R136.pdf

(4) United Nations General Assembly. *Visit to the United Kingdom of Great Britain and Northern Ireland Report of the Special Rapporteur on Extreme Poverty and Human Rights*, Bristol: University of Bristol, 2019. https://undocs.org/A/HRC/41/39/Add.1

(5) *Recent History of UK Child Poverty*. Child Poverty Action Group, no date. https://cpag.org.uk/recent-history-uk-child-poverty

(6) Office for National Statistics. *Households Below Average Income: For Financial Years ending 1995 to 2020*. London: Department for Work and Pensions, 2021. https://www.gov.uk/government/statistics/households-below-average-income-for-financial-years-ending-1995-to-2020

(7) Low Pay Commission, *20 years of the National Minimum Wage. A History of the UK Minimum Wage and its Effects*. London: Low Pay Commission, 2019. https://assets.publishing.service.gov.uk/government/uploads/system/uploads/attachment_data/file/790910/20_years_of_the_National_Minimum_Wage_-_a_history_of_the_UK_minimum_wage_and_its_effects.pdf

(8) Clegg, D., 'The demise of tax credits', *The Political Quarterly*, 2015, 86, 493–499. https://doi.org/10.1111/1467-923X.12203

(9) Tomlinson, S., 'New Labour and education', *Children & Society*, 17, 195–204. 10 March 2006. https://doi.org/10.1002/CHI.764

(10) Dwyer, P., 'Creeping conditionality in the UK: from welfare rights to conditional entitlements?'. *The Canadian Journal of Sociology*, Spring, 29 (2), 2004. *Special Issue on Social Policy: Canadian and International Perspectives* (Spring, 2004), 265–287.

(11) *What is Welfare Conditionality? Welfare Conditionality, Sanctions, Support and Behaviour Change*. http://www.welfareconditionality.ac.uk/about-our-research/what-is-welfare-conditionality

(12) Office for National Statistics, *The 2008 Recession 10 years on. A Decade after the Beginning of the Recession, How Has the UK Economy Recovered?* London: Office for National Statistics, 2018. https://www.ons.gov.uk/economy/grossdomesticproductgdp/articles/the2008recession10yearson/2018-04-30

(13) Kenway, P., *Back to the 20th Century: Our Child Poverty Disaster*, London: National Policy Institute, 2021. https://www.npi.org.uk/blog/income-and-poverty/back-20th-century-our-child-poverty-disaster/

(14) Machin, R., 'The professional and ethical dilemmas of the two-child limit for child tax credit and Universal Credit', *Ethics and Social Welfare*, 11 (4) 404–411, 2017.

(15) Policy in Practice, *The Impact of Welfare Reform on Child Vulnerability*, London: Policy in Practice, 2019. https://policyinpractice.co.uk/wp-content/uploads/The-impact-of-welfare-reform-on-child-vulnerability-pub-12May2019.pdf

(16) Social Metrics Commission, *Measuring Poverty 2020: A Report of the Social Metrics Commission*, London: Social Metrics Commission, 2020. https://socialmetricscommission.org.uk/wp-content/uploads/2020/06/Measuring-Poverty-2020-Web.pdf

(17) Social Metrics Commission, as above (16).

(18) Social Metrics Commission, as above (16).

(19) Institute of Health Equity, *Health Equity in England. The Marmot Review 10 Years On*. London: Health Foundation, 2020. https://www.instituteofhealthequity.org/resources-reports/marmot-review-10-years-on/the-marmot-review-10-years-on-full-report.pdf

(20) Arora, S. K., Shah, D., Chaturvedi, S., and Gupta, P., 'Defining and measuring vulnerability in young people', *Indian Journal of Community Medicine*, 40 (3) 193–197, 2015. https://doi.org/10.4103/0970-0218.158868

(21) Bennett, D.L, Mason, K. E, Schlüter, D. K. *et al*, 'Trends in inequalities in children looked after in England between 2004 and 2019: A local area ecological analysis.' *BMJ Open*, 10: e041774, 2020. doi:10.1136/bmjopen–2020–041774

(22) Bywaters, P., Bunting, L. and Davidson, G., *The Relationship Between Poverty, Child Abuse and Neglect: An Evidence Review*. York: Joseph Rowntree Foundation, 2016.

(23) Buttle UK, *The State of Child Poverty 2021: The Ongoing Impact of COVID Crisis on Families and Young People Living in Poverty*. London: Buttle UK, 2021 https://buttleuk.org/news/news–list/state-of-child-poverty-2021/

(24) Schweiger, G., 'Ethics, poverty and children's vulnerability', *Ethics and Social Welfare*, 13 (3) 288–301, 26 March, 2019. doi:10.1080/17496535.2019.1593480

(25) Beddoe, L. and Keddell, E., 'Informed outrage: tackling shame and stigma in poverty education in social work', *Ethics and Social Welfare*, 10 (2) 149–162, 2016. doi: 10.1080/17496535.2016.1159775

(26) Beddoe, L. and Keddell, E., as above (25).

(27) Morris, K., White, S., Doherty, P., and Warwick, L., 'Out of time: theorizing family in social work practice', *Child & Family Social Work*, 22, 51–60, 2017. https://dx.doi.org/10.1111/cfs.12257

(28) Department of Health, *Framework for the Assessment of Children in Need and their Families*. London: The Stationery Office, 2000.

(29) Gupta, A., 'Poverty and child neglect: the elephant in the room?' *Families, Relationships and Societies*, 6 (1) 21–36, 2017.

(30) Hood, R., Goldacre, A., Gorin, S. and Bywaters, P., 'Screen, ration and churn: demand management and the crisis in children's social care', *British Journal of Social Work,* 50 (3) 868–889, 2020. https://doi.org/10.1093/bjsw/bcz035

(31) Pridd, Helen, 'Dire poverty in North-East England "driving many more children into care"', *The Guardian*, 28 July, 2021.

(32) Ofsted, *Main Findings: Children's Social Care in England 2021* [online] London: Ofsted, 2021. https://www.gov.uk/government/statistics/childrens-social-care-data-in-england-2021/main-findings-childrens-social-care-in-england-2021

(33) Morris, K., Mason, W., Bywaters, P. *et al*, 'Social work, poverty, and child welfare interventions.' *Child & Family Social Work*, 23, 364–372, 2018.

(34) O'Brien, M., 'Social justice: alive and well (partly) in social work practice?' *International Social Work*, 54m (2) 174–190, 2010.

(35) BASW and Child Welfare Inequalities Projects, *Anti-Poverty Practice Guide for Social Work*, Birmingham: BASW, p.14, 2019.

(36) Krumo-Nevo, Michal, 'Poverty-aware social work: a paradigm for social work practice with people in poverty', *British Journal of Social Work*, pp. 1793–1808, 2016; and O'Brien, M., as above.

(37) Gupta, A., 'Learning from others: An autoethnographic exploration of children and families social work, poverty and the capability approach', *Qualitative Social Work*, 16, 2–17 (4), 449–464, 2015.

(38) Saar-Heiman, Y. and Gupta, A. The poverty-aware paradigm for child protection: A critical framework for policy and practice. *The British Journal of Social Work*, 50 (4), pp.1167–1184, 2020.

Dewanckel, L., Decoene, J., Van Beveren, L., Roose, R. and Roets, G., Dealing with risk in situations of poverty: when complexity in frontline practice becomes wallpaper for organisational policy. *European Journal of Social Work*, pp.1–13, 2021.

(39) BASW and CWIP, as above (35).

(40) Department of Health Northern Ireland, *Anti-Poverty Practice Framework for Social Work in Northern Ireland*, 2018. Available at: https://www.health-ni.gov.uk/sites/default/files/publications/health/Povertyframework.pdf

(41) Feldman, G., 'Towards a relational approach to poverty in social work: Research and practice considerations', *British Journal of Social Work*, pp1705–1722, 2019.

(42) Krumo-Nevo, M., as above (36).

(43) Saar-Heiman, Y. and Gupta, A., The poverty-aware paradigm for child protection: A critical framework for policy and practice. *The British Journal of Social Work*, 50(4), pp.1167–1184, 2020.

Dewanckel, L., Decoene, J., Van Beveren, L., Roose, R. and Roets, G., Dealing with risk in situations of poverty: when complexity in frontline practice becomes wallpaper for organisational policy. *European Journal of Social Work*, pp.1–13, 2021.

(44) Dewanckel, L., Decoene, J., Van Beveren, L., Roose, R. and Roets, G., Dealing with risk in situations of poverty: when complexity in frontline practice becomes wallpaper for organisational policy. *European Journal of Social Work*, pp.1–13, 2021.

BASW and CWIP, *Anti-Poverty Practice Guide for Social Work*, British Association of Social Workers, 2019.

Department of Health NI, *Anti-Poverty Practice Framework for Social Work in Northern Ireland*, 2018 Available at: https://www.health-ni.gov.uk/sites/default/files/publications/health/Povertyframework.pdf

(45) BASW and CWIP, 2019, p.18 as above (35).

(46) Krumo-Nevo, M., p.1081 as above (36).

(47) Department of Health Northern Ireland, 2018 p.26 as above (40).

(48) Saar-Heiman, Y. and Gupta, A., The poverty-aware paradigm for child protection: A critical framework for policy and practice. *The British Journal of Social Work*, 50(4), pp.1167–1184, 2020.

Feldman, G., Towards a relational approach to poverty in social work: research and practice considerations, *British Journal of Social Work*, 1705–1722, 2019.

Department of Health NI, *Anti-Poverty Practice Framework for Social Work in Northern Ireland*, 2018. Available at: https://www.health-ni.gov.uk/sites/default/files/publications/health/Povertyframework.pdf

(49) Krumo-Nevo, M., Poverty-aware social work: a paradigm for social work practice with people in poverty, *British Journal of Social Work*, 1793–1808, 2016.

Department of Health NI *Anti-Poverty Practice Framework for Social Work in Northern Ireland*, 2018. Available at: https://www.health-ni.gov.uk/sites/default/files/publications/health/Povertyframework.pdf

Saar-Heiman, Y. and Gupta, A., 2020. The poverty-aware paradigm for child protection: A critical framework for policy and practice. *British Journal of Social Work*, 50 (4), pp.1167–1184, 2020.

(50) Krumo-Nevo, M., p.1805 as above; and BASW and CWIP, p.17 as above.

(51) BASW and CWIP, *Anti-Poverty Practice Guide for Social Work*, British Association of Social Workers, 2019.

Saar-Heiman, Y. and Gupta, A., The poverty-aware paradigm for child protection: A critical framework for policy and practice. *British Journal of Social Work*, 50 (4), pp.1167–1184, 2020.

(52) BASW and CWIP, p.17 as above (35).

(53) BASW and CWIP, as above (35); Department of Health Northern Ireland, as above (36); and Saar-Heiman, Y. and Gupta, A., as above.

(54) BASW and CWIP, as above (35).

(55) BASW and CWIP, *Anti-Poverty Practice Guide for Social Work*, British Association of Social Workers, 2019.

Gupta, A., Learning from others: an autoethnographic exploration of children and families social work, poverty and the capability approach, *Qualitative Social Work*, 16 (4), 449–464, 2017.

(56) Dewanckel *et al*, p.3 as above.

(57) Department of Health, Northern Ireland, as above (36).

(58) Krumer-Nevo, M.; Weiss-Gal, I. and Monnickendam, M. 'Poverty-aware social work practice: a conceptual framework for social work education', *Journal of Social Work Education*, 45 (2) 225–243, 2009.

(59) Department of Health Northern Ireland, as above (36).

(60) Gottfried Schweiger, as above (24).

Art project between Plymouth University and children in care

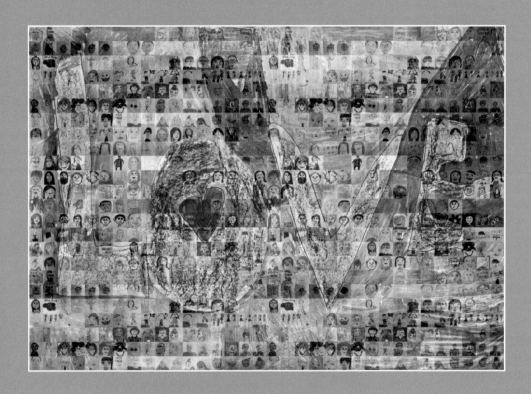

Producing a montage and creating the word LOVE which is what the children wanted to be central to their experience in care.

CHAPTER 11

Shaping a New Path for Children's Services

Chris Hanvey

Introduction

In August 1973 a public enquiry began in Brighton to investigate the death of Maria Colwell, a 7-year-old who had died of multiple injuries caused by her step-father, William Kepple. During her brief life Maria had been known to her school teacher, her GP, the NSPCC, the recently formed East Sussex social services department, and other professionals. There had been worried reports from neighbours to the NSPCC and, during the last nine months of her life, 30 concerns raised about her welfare from a number of people (1).

But there was an added dimension to the outcry over Maria's tragic death. Only two years earlier, and following a report by Sir Frederick (later Lord) Seebohm (2), local authority social services departments had been established to bring together a range of separate agencies such as children's departments, welfare services, education welfare and child guidance, and mental health social work services, and the social work provided by health departments. Instead of the long acknowledged lack of co-ordination between these organisations, which had previously existed, there would now be 'one door on which to knock', through which children and adults would effortlessly enter, regardless of their problems. And yet, scarcely two years later this still brave new world of 'generic' social services was perceived to be failing. The safety net of care was revealed to have gaping holes.

Cut to 2021 and a serious case review into a six-year-old, thrown from the tenth storey viewing platform at Tate Modern in London. His attacker, Jonty Bravery, was 17 and had been diagnosed with autism when he was five. But the review acknowledged there was a clear 'lack of join up between different elements of support' (3). He had spent periods of his life being moved between psychiatric units, specialist residential schools, and hotels. As the review further recorded, 'the mismatch between [his] needs and available provision ran through the whole case' (4). Almost 50 years after than the Maria Colwell enquiry, services for young people are still not integrated or joined up to provide for children's complex needs. What this chapter explores is how such integration might be achieved (5).

Of course, these two tragic examples examine children's services through the prism of things going badly wrong. An even-handed approach needs to look, also, at the many improvements to children's lives that equally have been made. In many ways it is the best of times and the worst of times. It is the age of limitless information; it is the age of borderless social media. It is the epoch of wide opportunities; it is the era of unprecedented competition. It is a century of healthier, better educated children; it is a time of disturbing sexual abuse, easy access to pornography and unlimited advertising. Young people have all before them, but inhabit a hothouse of social pressure. Of no age group are these factors truer than for the young, growing up today both in the UK and in other European countries.

So when we point specifically to Maria Colwell, the sad roll call of subsequent child protection tragedies which followed her death or the failure to provide adequately for the mental and physical needs of young people, what exactly are the problems we are seeking to remedy?

The emphasis, in this chapter, is very much on children in need and it is important we are clear what these needs are. There have been countless classifications of need, aiming either at a generic index or that based on the analysis of a specific professional group. It is best characterised by a single pyramid, then subdivided horizontally in a range of slightly differing ways. Basic divisions are between intensive help, medium support and signposting to agencies offering additional guidance. For example, if we take a child with mental health needs, tier 1 or base of the pyramid could be a single referral through primary care, such as the GP or health visitor. Tier 2 would be to a specific mental health worker for, say, counselling or similar skilled support. Tier 3 would be a referral to a specialist child and adolescent worker and tier 4 to a specialist day or in-patient unit. In the case of children with significant health issues, the tiers move from support available through general practice all the way up to level 4 where intervention may include palliative care.

This chapter's emphasis is on children within tiers 3 and 4, where the level of intervention needed – from whatever agency – is relatively high. These are children whose health, social care or educational needs, for example, are severe and where they and their carers will probably require contact with a range of agencies. It is here that the argument for 'joined up services' is at its most acute.

Integrated care

It is interesting that debates about integrated services – which are common currency within adult care – have largely escaped services for children. There are two main reasons for this. First, the argument for greater integration of adult services or rather those for elderly people between health and social care was largely driven by the necessity to get elderly patients out of hospitals and back into the community. 'Bed-blocking', as it is infelicitously described, was a powerful incentive. But, second, integrating all of the services upon which tier 3 and tier 4 children depend – health, social care, education, youth and mental health services, housing, income support and the voluntary sector – is far more complex than for elderly services and demands a much greater degree of 'joined up' thinking. A simple example will suffice.

When asked what was one of the most common referrals to a children's A&E department, a paediatric colleague immediately said 'asthma'. Children living in poor quality, damp, often rented accommodation, were admitted with respiratory problems, patched up and discharged, only to see the whole process repeated several weeks or months later. The consequence of this was lost school time and therefore poorer exam results and possible knock-on effects later for chances in the job market. To address just this issue required a coming together of housing, income support, education, social care and health services, to prevent an endless cycle of hospital re-referrals. And yet, 50 years after the Seebohm report, 'wrap around childcare' or the concept of 'the team around the child' (6) is more honoured in the breach than the observance. And this lack of integration is reflected not only at a local level but all the way up to government departments.

As Helen Seaford wryly noted:

> 'The child moves through Whitehall growing and
> shrinking like Alice: in the Department of Health
> she is a small potential victim, at the Treasury and
> Department of Education a growing but silent unit
> of investment, but at the Home Office a huge and
> threatening yob.' (7)

This is not to say that there haven't been previous attempts to bring
services together, but they rarely cross the whole gamut of children's
needs.

One of the most successful, if partial successes of integration, has been
the establishment of Multi-Agency Safeguarding Hubs (MASH) in a
number of parts of England. Aimed at integrating child protection
services, the composition of MASH staff varies, but the core is likely to
include social work, education, and health workers, and the police, with
some hubs also choosing to include probation, the ambulance service,
youth justice, and housing. What these MASH provide is a single point
of entry for child protection services, which might be via letters, emails
or telephone calls. They permit the sharing of information between
agencies, allow referrals to be triaged, facilitate early intervention and
manage children through rapidly convened multi-agency case
discussions.

Once a referral is received there is usually a search across the various
databases, to see what is known of the child and carers and to provide
the basis for a meeting of all the agencies who might have an
involvement (8). This then allows a decision to be made rapidly as to
which should be the lead agency and what action is necessary.
Evidence from the London MASH hub indicated that they have the
potential to develop more effective multi-agency working than more
usual arrangements (9). Two factors are particularly important. First, that
MASH schemes have the potential for improvements in partnership
communication and information sharing. Second, and this is perhaps
even more significant, that this kind of multi-agency working creates a
new and shared culture that is different from the culture of a single
organisation. Here the whole is not only greater than the sum of its
parts, but fundamentally different from the parts themselves.

Attention has been devoted to MASH hubs because they demonstrate
that even in a complex area, such as child protection, where tribal
loyalties and interdisciplinary disputes are great, it is possible to achieve
'joined up' working between agencies. Another established model, this

time for child and adolescent mental health services, was the formation of CAMHS in 1995. Here again, they are based on the concept of multi-disciplinary teams, with psychiatrists, psychologists, social workers and therapists offering occupational and family therapy, focused solely on the mental health needs of young people.

Shaping Children's Services (10) provides descriptions of a number of national and international attempts to bring children's agencies to work together, whether in the area of pre-school services, school age education, children's centres, youth justice, or services for children and young people with disabilities. What remains missing is a generic model of integration which could be rolled out across the UK and would embrace all of those agencies which individually cater for aspects of children's needs. What the remaining part of this chapter outlines is what such a model would look like.

Two provisos are necessary. First, what is proposed is not a 'quick fix' but would take several years to introduce, research, modify and bed down. Second, the model is based on the following principles:

- It should be pre-eminently child focused, turning 'wrap around care', from a lazy slogan to a reality.

- It needs to be adaptable enough to fit in with the demographics of specific neighbourhoods.

- It needs to reflect the complexity of the present funding environment – with slate, voluntary and private sector providers.

- It should encompass health, social care, education, leisure, youth services, police, housing the voluntary and private sectors and the benefit agencies.

- It should have a genuinely preventive agenda, aiming to intervene early to stop problems developing.

- It should function according to those pyramids of need, where children with the greatest problems receive the most support.

- It should not involve further major reorganisation of any of the contributing services.

Children's services teams

At the end of, and immediately following, the Second World War there was a reform of welfare and health services on a scale never previously seen. It led to the establishment of the NHS, bold housing plans, a new

Education Act, and an overhaul of income support for poorer families. It was brought about because of the urgent need to build a progressive Britain and put in place a structure which would help the country re-build. It is my contention that we have now arrived at a point where services for children are so dispersed and, in some cases so dysfunctional that change on the same scale as the post war reforms is now needed.

At the heart of these proposals is the establishment of children's services teams (CSTs) which will have, as their starting point, the allocation of staff from health, social care, education, leisure, housing and so on into a new multi-disciplinary team. But this is not about creating new, rigid roles but a model that permits separate professional groups to come together and forge a common identity to meet local need. It is closer to a secondment in which multi-disciplinary staff work together within the umbrella of the CSTs – very much in line with the organisation of some of the MASH hubs outlined above.

It is proposed that each locality will have a multi-disciplinary CST. This will serve differing populations dependent on whether they are in rural or urban areas. Each CST will fit in to existing local government and health structures- whether based on districts, towns or cities, and will provide a good workable fit without creating a whole new organisational tier. Each locality will have a central CST administration and operational base, where professionals working across the whole spectrum of prevention, support and help for children will come together. This will include representations of primary care, health visitors, district nurses, community paediatricians, children's social workers, school representatives, voluntary and private sector providers of services, housing and housing association workers, school nurses, occupational and speech therapists, CAMHS staff, those involved in income support, the police and youth justice services, and those who run local leisure services for children. The listing of so many professions forcefully makes the point about the challenges integration faces for children, as opposed to elderly people.

Professionals who become part of CSTs will form two distinct groups – those who are full-time CST team members, such as community paediatricians, children's social workers, educational support liaison workers, and health visitors. The second group will be engaged with the CST on a part-time basis and will include housing, leisure or income support workers, for example. For this second group, they may also have responsibilities for adult care and, therefore, will be brought in when additional support services or professional expertise for children and their families is required.

Bringing teams of disparate professionals together is not without considerable challenge. For example, a locality CST team will realistically not be able to include representations from each school or GP practice it serves. There will need to be some system of delegation in which individuals represent their wider constituency or professional grouping. They will then take on the responsibility to both refer children to the central team and take back any recommendations and actions, to ensure they are implemented. At the same time it is proposed that when there are serious child protection concerns for a child, then the relevant GP and school, for example, will be fully represented.

The location of CSTs is challenging, with a number of potential solutions. The model proposes that they will become focal points for children and young people within their local community. Large schools with the necessary space could, theoretically, provide an attractive location for CSTs. They would have an immediate link with many of the children who require additional support and, of course, because education is a universal service, they are non-stigmatising.

Equally free from stigma are GP health centres, which increasingly combine a range of functions such as clinics, support groups, crèches and other services. Another option would be the 'one-stop shop', developed by some local authorities, where libraries, health clinics and housing, for example, operate from the same public-facing building. All of these provide universal, non-stigmatising options but, more realistically, the solution may lie in newly commissioned buildings, capable of accommodating the multi-disciplinary CST team. Space will inevitably be needed for baby clinics, interview and consultancy rooms for social workers and paediatricians to examine children, interview suites for the investigation of child abuse, and space for advice sessions for, say, housing or income support. Ensuring that CST centres are also the places where new babies are formally registered would ensure that there was an initial contact with all new-borns. This concept is one of purpose-built centres, designed with children in mind, having reception desks at child height, toys very much in evidence and a welcoming friendly environment, conducive to warm interactions between children, carers and professionals. The vision is of a national network of CST child-centred buildings, welcoming to families and attractive places to work.

It is further proposed that the CST would operate a hub-and-spoke model. As well as the central location of the team in a single place, there would be spokes or sub-offices (especially in rural areas) where, for example, babies could be weighed and examined and young people interviewed. They must be accessible to the local population, with good IT and communication facilities.

There are four further elements that are essential to the introduction of the CST model:

- pooled budgets

- a common referral and assessment process

- the allocation of a named person for each child

- the development of technology that would securely allow the exchange of information and better diagnostic and treatment tools.

Pooling budgets is essential to the CST. The idea is not new and was proposed in relation to the development of Sure Start centres. Pooled budgets allow a more holistic and preventive approach to working with families and help to break down the silo mentality in which departments are single minded about conserving resources. The pooled budgets would also permit the commissioning of those additional services which the localities feel to be necessary for their specific populations.

The vision of a comprehensive and shared referral and assessment process, though paved with good intentions, remains currently unrealised. Crucial to CSTs is a two-part referral form which would contain a mix of generic information (part 1) and specialist (part 2). The goal of a shared, generic referral form, containing data on children which all agencies can use is a prize well worth fighting for. It would also provide an initial indication of the level of need – as outlined earlier. Need is a complex concept and should embrace the child's living situation, family and social relations, social and anti-social behaviour, physical and psychological health, education and employment. Each of these 'touch points' needs addressing if a child is to be assessed holistically – the whole point behind the establishment of CSTs. However, it has to be acknowledged that establishing a shared database for CSTs will present one of the largest and, so far, illusive challenges for the success of an integrated childcare system.

Summary

We need stand-alone CSTs, located in purpose-built hubs-and-spokes with a shared referral and assessment process and the ability to access a common database. Each referral will be seen by two different childcare professionals from the core CST team and there will be a nominated named person or lead profession who will become the principal point of contact for the child. Such a post was established in Scotland in 2017, following the introduction of the Children and Young People (Scotland) Act 2014, with a named person for every child. Clearly, the allocation to a specific discipline will be determined by the child's primary needs. But one huge benefit of the CST will partly lie in the ability of the named person to draw in other professions within the same team and building.

It will also be necessary for each CST to have a nominated head or director and it is envisaged that this would be a statutory function, with the head determined locally. So, he or she could come from a range of disciplines, for example, health, social care or education representatives located within the central team. The head would carry the major responsibility for commissioning both mainstream and additional services and produce an annual plan of work.

The last piece of this administrative jigsaw would be a local management board, made up of health, social care, education and other statutory providers, together with stakeholders and community representatives. It would also be important that public health specialists were fully engaged in the management board, in order to advise on national and local demographics, social and health trends. Not only would the board hold the CST head to account but produce a published annual report. This, again, would be a statutory document that reflected a combination of local and national priorities and conformed to a national framework of good childcare practice. Each CST would deliver a combination of local and national priorities and have a statutory obligation to report achievement to central government against national and local priorities on an annual basis.

The proposed introduction of CSTs is not, as has been stated, a quick fix. Locating buildings, putting teams together, sorting out referral and assessment forms, operating from the same location and with a shared database will take time to evolve and implement. It will equally mean an almost unprecedented degree of political consensus. Too often, childcare development in the UK has been characterised by short-term initiatives, each triggered by political expediency or a need to demonstrate that action is quickly being taken to address a current crisis. But CSTs would need stability to evolve and an awareness that it will take time for the implementation of what could be a world class integrated children's service. What is needed is the same vision, drive and shared goals that were exhibited in the darkest days of the Second World War.

If Covid has demonstrated anything, it is the need for integrated services. But current developments in childcare show a dilution rather than a concentration on the holistic needs of children. CAMHS services, for example, are severely stretched, schools struggle to meet the mental health needs of pupils, voluntary and private sector providers sometimes compete to run what were previously local authority services and the number of children in care awaiting foster or adoptive homes has grown considerably.

It is now essential we build a first class joined up children's service that mirrors the current debate about integrated elderly services, and fully recognises the role of the professions and totally engages them in looking holistically at the needs of children and young people. For, as Nelson Mandela said in 1995,

> 'There can be no keener revelation of a society's soul than the way it treats its children.'

References

(1) Department of Health and Social Security, *Report of the Committee of Inquiry into the Care and Supervision Provided in Relation To Maria Colwell*. London: HMSO, 1974.

(2) Home Department, the Secretary of State for Education and Science, the Minister of Housing and Local Government, and the Minister of Health, *Report of the Committee on Local Authority and Allied Personal Social Services*, Cmnd 3703, London: HMSO, 1968.

(3) Local Safeguarding Children Partnership, *Serious Case Review: 'David'*, London: London Borough of Hammersmith and Fulham & Royal Borough of Kensington and Chelsea, Westminster, 2021.

(4) As (3) above.

(5) For a longer exploration of these ideas see Hanvey, C., *Shaping Children's Services*. London: Routledge, 2019.

(6) (5) as above.

(7) Seaford, H., 'Children and childhood: perceptions and realities', *The Political Quarterly*, 72 (4) 454–465, 2001.

(8) Multi-Agency Working and Information Sharing Project, *Final Report*. London: Home Office, 2014.

(9) Crockett, R., Gilchrist, G., Davies, J. *et al*, *Assessing the Early Impact of Multi-Agency Safeguarding Hubs (MASH) in London*. Commissioned by the London Councils, 2013.

(10) (5) as above.